Are You Managing
Your Health?

ABOUT THE AUTHORS

Dr H Beric Wright is Allied Dunbar's consultant on health and retirement. Now himself retired, he was the founder of the Institute of Directors Medical Centre (which later became the BUPA Medical Centre) and a Director of BUPA until 1985. He has written and lectured extensively on health matters and believes that in holistic terms we can largely control our own medical destiny. He is co-author of the *Allied Dunbar Retirement Planning Guide*.

Dr Patricia Last (who contributed the chapter 'Women's Concerns') is particularly well-qualified to write on health and fitness. As the Director of Women's Screening at BUPA, she knows only too well the benefits that good health maintenance can bring.

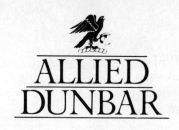

ALLIED DUNBAR

Are You Managing Your Health?

by
Dr H Beric Wright
MB FRCS MFOM

THE INDUSTRIAL SOCIETY

First published 1991 by
The Industrial Society
Robert Hyde House
48 Bryanston Square
London
WIH 7LN
Tel: 071–262–2401

ISBN 0 85290 902 0

Illustrations by Hal

No responsibility for loss occasioned to any person acting or refraining from action as a result of the material in this book can be accepted by the author, The Industrial Society or Allied Dunbar. The views and opinions of The Industrial Society and Allied Dunbar may not necessarily coincide with some of the views and opinions expressed in this book which are solely those of the author and no endorsement of them by The Industrial Society or Allied Dunbar should be inferred.

British Library Cataloguing in Publications Data
Wright, H. Beric (Henry Beric)
  Are you managing your health?
  1. **Man. Health**
  I. **Title II. Allied Dunbar Assurance plc**

Allied Dunbar Assurance plc
Allied Dunbar Centre
Swindon SN1 1EL
Tel: 0793 514514

Typeset by Acūté, Stroud, Glos.
Printed and bound by Biddles Ltd, Guildford, Surrey.

'Tis in ourselves that we are thus or thus. Our bodies are our gardens to which our wills are gardeners

Iago
Othello, Act 1 Sc 3

THE INDUSTRIAL SOCIETY

The Industrial Society promotes the involvement of all people in their work in order to increase the effectiveness of organisations and the satisfaction of individuals. The Society is a leading advisory and training body in Britain in the management of people and industrial relations. It is independent and self-financing, providing services which include in-company advice and training, courses and conferences, information, publications, audio-visual training programmes and a quarterly magazine.

Its staff includes 200 management advisers with wide, practical experience in industry, commerce and the public services. For more information, please contact the Society's principal office at *Robert Hyde House, 48 Bryanston Square, London W1H 7LN Tel 071 262 2401.*

ALLIED DUNBAR

Allied Dunbar is one of Britain's largest financial groups, offering services which include life assurance, personal pensions and unit trust investment. With more than one million clients and over £8 billion funds under management, Allied Dunbar has been recognised as one of the leading growth companies and innovators in the UK personal Financial Services industry.

There are over 7,000 Allied Dunbar people, comprising a large professional sales force backed by a team of managers and support staff. Allied Dunbar's business success is based on sound management practices and the commitment of all its people.

CONTENTS

CONTENTS

FOREWORD ———————————

'Management' means many things to many people and it has a variety of definitions. One which perhaps gets close to the mark is to describe management as the utilisation of available resources to get the best possible performance out of ourselves and out of others.

Resources, of course, should not just refer to buildings, plant, machinery, money, and so on. It refers to people themselves as they are our most valuable resource.

Consequently, health is important – and it is as important to the people we manage as it is to ourselves and our families. Fortunately, healthy living has now become more than just a passing fad and there is a growing awareness that the health of the nation is as much in our own hands as those of our political masters.

My own particular interest is in mental health. It is very much a 'cinderella' subject but that ignores the fearful price paid by industry and commerce each year due to the lack of mental well-being in our employees – and in ourselves. When I agreed to Chair the Mental Health Foundation 40th Anniversary Appeal, it was on the basis that more had to be done to support the cause of mental health in this country. By the end of 1989, we had made good progress – over half of our total of £5 million had been raised and we had a pledge from the Government to work in partnership with the Foundation to consolidate new advances in both research and care.

Allied Dunbar have played a leading role in this appeal and

I'm delighted that they are donating the proceeds of this book to help us meet our target.

Doctor Wright's thesis is that, to a very great extent, good health is in our own hands. You may feel that much of it is nothing other than plain common sense but, as Alistair Graham, the Director of the Industrial Society, said in the foreword to the sister volume *Are You Managing?*, the application of common sense is very often a prerequisite to good management.

Sir David Plastow

PREFACE

As a leading financial services organisation, it is perhaps a little unusual in some people's eyes that Allied Dunbar should devote so much to the pursuit of health and physical well-being. Nevertheless, throughout our culture, there is a strong streak of belief in encouraging the well-being not only of the fit and healthy but also of the less fortunate.

Our four charitable organisations, for example, have a long history of actively supporting the welfare of those not able to look after themselves. We are enthusiastic supporters of the Mental Health Foundation 40th Anniversary Appeal, and our range of books contains titles on health and fitness.

More recently, we are delighted to play a major role in the Allied Dunbar National Fitness Survey which sets out to take the pulse of the nation's general health, the first such survey ever carried out in the United Kingdom.

Beric Wright has not only had wide medical experience in surgery, screening and health promotion, he was also a Senior Manager in a large organisation. This almost unique range of experience gives him a wide overview of medical and managerial options on which his forthright views – with which we do not necessarily always agree – certainly stimulate thought.

We are pleased to be associated with this, the second title in the Allied Dunbar management range, and we hope that it will benefit the reader as much as it will benefit the Mental Health Foundation.

A P Leitch
Deputy Chairman
Allied Dunbar Assurance plc

INTRODUCTION ──────────

IN SEARCH OF WELL-BEING

In 1958, having worked as a surgeon overseas for nearly six years and thoroughly enjoyed it, the time came to resettle in England, largely because of our children's education. I could afford to be off work for three months, so had a good European holiday and then went job hunting. I had decided that I was unlikely to get the kind of surgical job I wanted but I had had some experience of administration (of hospitals), of administrative politics (a woolly-minded oil company hierarchy) and occupational health.

Through a piece of serendipity, which involved John Marsh, then at The Industrial Society, and the late Sir Richard Powell of the Institute of Directors, I persuaded the latter organisation that they should take on a doctor, for a trial period, to look for possible work-related problems among their members.

At this time the Institute of Directors had the largest single BUPA group and BUPA itself was concerned about the claims experience of this group which was 120 per cent of premium income. This seemed to be a marvellous opportunity to learn something of the epidemiology of the group, i.e. the incidence and nature of their diseases. With the guidance of a distinguished professor of epidemiology, we pulled out thousands of files of Institute members, logged their claims' experience and tried to compare it with a control group.

1

Sadly, however, what we found was, firstly, that doctors filling up the claim forms used euphemisms to describe the diseases; secondly, the directors claimed for every penny they thought they could get, and thirdly, the doctors, knowing they were treating directors, upped their fees.

But for me, the most interesting finding was that the claims' experience of directors' partners and children was far higher than the control group. 'Ah ha', I thought to myself, 'unhappy, neglected husbands and wives, trailing their pains up and down Harley Street'. I stored all this away for later digestion as it was at that time unpublishable, although it led to a nice bit of friction between the two organisations.

This was, of course, thirty years ago. At that time, 1958-60, the perceived wisdom was that duodenal ulcers were the business person's disease, probably because all good American tycoons were thought to have one, or even two. The one-ulcer manager in the two-ulcer job was a popular stereotype. But when we looked at what British managers suffered from, it was coronary thrombosis (CHD) and not ulcers. Indeed, the UK was top of the international coronary league, headed, it seemed, by managers.

In fact, both here and in the States, people were starting to be concerned about CHD and beginning to look for causes. In parallel with this interest, the study of stress was gathering momentum and the stressed executive became a cult figure. All the best executives were expected to be stressed, particularly so by their families.

This inevitably led me in two directions which were to dominate the rest of my medical work. The first was that in order to be able to understand and counsel this somewhat harrassed and bemused occupational group, one had to be interested in, know about and understand their problems. What better place to do this than the Institute of Directors? So I became concerned about what these people did, from tea and coffee tasting to bullion broking, and this led, inevitably, to examining the dynamics, working practices and traditions of individual companies.

Much more critically, however, it became clear early on that more than just work was involved. Much of the conflict and anxiety came from home life. We decided, therefore,

2

that to analyse or understand anyone's lifestyle we had to look at work, home and leisure and then relate any problems to the symptoms. We were not interested in diseases or symptoms *per se* (which annoyed patients enormously, especially those who arrived with lists of symptoms) but we were concerned with the effects of lifestyle.

Secondly, and intimately related, was my growing interest in the understanding of stress and the psychosomatic (mind and body) approach to ease and dis-ease. This taught me that not only did mind and body inter-react to produce dis-ease – which was traditionally called illness – but that this dis-ease represented a spectrum of symptoms from the obviously organic (appendicitis, perhaps) to the clearly emotional states of depression and anxiety (i.e. mood change could produce the physical and/or behavioural changes which we recognised as illness). But in those days, physical disease was socially acceptable whereas mental disease, particularly in its less flagrant forms, was barely comprehended and not regarded as genuine. This interpretation was based on the general belief that symptoms without an obvious organic cause were imaginary. Now, however, all symptoms are accepted as being real to the patient and hence a call for help.

This experience made it clear that one had to look at the whole person and their lifestyle and not just the body system to which the symptoms related nor the slice of their life from which they thought it might come. This approach is now called holism and the role of the mind-body tug-of-war is accepted. The word 'health' actually comes from the Greek word meaning 'wholeness'.

My mother was a doctor who was largely concerned with family planning, and she had a holistic approach to medicine, asking her patients about their husbands and families and often sending the latter to me, as I would send managers' wives to her. Also interesting was the relationship I had with the late John Tyzack, an enlightened management consultant. We would often swap 'patients' for companies, and vice versa. Sick companies produce stressed people.

Here it is important to make a vital point about stress which, as I have said, became a cult phrase. What caused confusion was that people did not realise that, in biological terms, challenge is the critical motivator of existence. There has to be something – a target – to live for; satisfaction comes from achieving the target. Challenge, then, is both essential and desirable but it is *not* stress.

Stress is what happens when the individual cannot, at a subconscious level, cope with the challenge and the resulting conflict produces the symptoms, or in general terms, the dis-ease. Stress is therefore a failure to cope, and not necessarily a sign of fatigue and overwork, although the latter do influence the stress threshold. *Stress is thus a manifestation of inability to cope and not of success.*

Individuals have a genetic inheritance which gives them attributes, body build and personality. As they grow up and develop, they acquire experience – personal, educational, social and cultural – which makes them into what they become. It is this unique personality, strong or weak, intro-vert or extrovert, bright or dim, that reacts with their environment, meets challenge or becomes stressed. What we cannot cope with is the key to dis-ease, which in turn must be related to an internal balancing system which determines both resistance and, in some way we do not yet understand, the symptoms we develop to 'solve our stress'.

All this leads one to ponder why some people never become ill and avoid the common conditions which infect others. In trying to help individuals to deal with their symptoms or a parent to cope with an ailing child, *why* they are getting these symptoms is at least as important as *what* is wrong with them.

A few overt causes of disease can easily be identified. Gene abnormalities, for instance, are responsible for Down's Syndrome and a large range of other diseases, like cystic fibrosis. Other gene abnormalities produce a failure to metabolise dietary and other fats, causing familial hyper-cholesterolaemia and coronary heart disease (CHD). Expo-sure to toxic substances – silica in coal dust, asbestos and various other chemicals, including tobacco smoke – produces either diseases like silicosis or lung or bladder cancer. Similarly, individuals who eat too much of the wrong foods, fats or too many calories, become vulnerable to disease, particularly to CHD and obesity, itself a common disease.

Less well known, but a national tragedy, is the fact that where you live and what work you do are increasingly significant determinants of mortality (death) and morbidity (sickness). Edwina Currie was right, although it got her into trouble, to point out the increased health risks for those who live in the North-East. Social classes IV and V have two to three times the CHD rate as social classes I and II, as well as a much higher general mortality and morbidity rate. These differences, and several others, are lifestyle related.

Enough is now known about the causes of common diseases to identify what are called risk factors. These include risks like inhaling tobacco smoke or eating the wrong diet, which should be very much a matter of personal option and therefore a matter of informed choice.

What this means is that at this stage in our societal evolution, individuals have to make a number of personal and family choices about their physical and emotional lifestyle that will significantly influence their health and well-being. In these terms, health is usefully defined as a state of physical, mental and social well-being. As this involves the whole person and the way in which they adjust their attributes (skills, personality and experience) to their aspirations or targets, anything that contributes to their morale and satisfaction will help to maintain or influence their inner balance.

What you believe in strongly has an influence, hopefully for good: thus, it is likely to be motivationally powerful, and beneficial. Traditional medical practice has its failures and as treatments become more powerful and possibly dangerous, there has recently developed a much greater sympathy for, interest in and availability of, alternative and complementary therapies, and several, like Spiritual Healing and Homeopathy, do have historical respectability.

It is vital for all of us to realise that, to a very large extent, we hold the key to our own and our family's health. We have to understand the options and make wise choices about our physical, emotional and working lives. Personal relationships are a critical area in this decision-taking network. How we bring up our children largely determines the kind of people they will become and determines their future physical and mental lifestyle. For example, their parents' divorce can have a significant influence on children, and more thought needs to be given to this, and to the effect of remarriage.

At long last, these changes have begun to have a profound effect on the attitude of doctors and patients to each other. Traditionally, professionals, like doctors and lawyers, have been allowed to determine the sort of service they think the consumers ought to have. But these are consumer services and the consumers are beginning to revolt. We want information, we want to be presented with options so that we can decide which course to take. We also want time to talk and we expect doctors to understand how our anxieties can lead, misleadingly perhaps, to us presenting physical symptoms, because these are traditionally more acceptable to the doctor. We do not necessarily want a prescription, a sick certificate or even an operation. We want our hang-ups to be explained and to be helped to come to terms with them. The current sea-change in doctor/patient expectations should do a great deal to improve real health.

Avoiding coronary heart disease, which still kills about 25 per cent of all men before retiring age and a growing number of women, has been central to our thinking on prevention of disease. There are a number of proven or accepted risk factors which increase vulnerability. They all, except the genetic ones, relate primarily to physical or mental lifestyle: diet, exercise, smoking and stress. The choices one makes and the diet to which one's children become accustomed will have a very profound effect on life expectancy and enjoyment. Also, the choices one makes about one's physical and mental lifestyle, career and relationships, can, one way or another, significantly increase or diminish life-expectancy and enjoyment.

In Britain, we have a relatively stable, well-adjusted and contented society with a high level of well-being reflected in high morale and satisfaction. It would appear that medicine *per se* has contributed rather little to this dramatic change.

As I drift into full retirement and look back on the evolution of my attitude to health and disease, two factors seem important. The first is that the balance within each of us depends on what we make of our lives and how we play the genetic and other cards we were dealt. Within these

parameters and helped by appropriate knowledge and understanding, we have to make choices that will determine our
well-being. Life will not necessarily be easy and the cards
may be stacked against us, but if we make the best of what we
have and manage to balance aspirations and attributes, we
ought to remain reasonably well.

The second factor is for doctors and the public to realise
that in terms of social well-being, the promotion of health is
at least as, and in my view more, important than the treatment
of disease. Building up well-being will increase immunity
and resistance, and minimise the need for drugs and surgery.
Health does appear to be manageable and depends on wellness
and well-being. The aim of this book is to suggest ways in
which personal, family and company health can be managed
successfully.

CHAPTER ONE

ATTITUDES TO
HEALTH

INTRODUCTION

In basic biological terms the expression of pain is a spontaneous and largely uncontrollable call for help. It has generally been the case that the sufferer has always had these calls for help answered, and so doctors, healers and medicine-men have always been highly regarded in society, despite the fact that up to the twentieth century they often had little effective help to offer. In society as a whole, the result of a genuine desire to help the disabled (and perhaps to limit guilt about not always being able to provide relief or cure), has led to being ill – or more colloquially 'off sick' – becoming institutionalised and respectable. The process of being ill can be summed up as follows:

- We take our symptoms to the doctor to gain access to the healing system.
- On the whole, society is prepared to support us in this 'search for a cure' by providing reasonable access to both the Health Service and to social benefits (in terms of sick pay).
- However, what often comes as rather a surprise is that, in terms of determining disability and the need for

relief, it is the individual and not the doctor who is the prime mover in defining illness.

• Therefore, it is obvious that the doctor and his or her hospital and other back-up services can only help once they are consulted.

Consequently, it is often the individual's attitude to symptoms (conditioned, of course, by basic social attitudes and the availability of medical services) that can be critical in defining disease. Obviously, this personal attitude is not relevant when the distress is overwhelming as with severe illness, acute pain or physical trauma, but in terms of willingness to go to work, seek advice on prevention or health assessment, or worry about possibly trivial symptoms, then individual and family motivation is often the critical factor.

Most personnel managers know that the level of sickness absence in a company is as much a measure of morale and motivation as it is of actual illness. If times are hard, either directly financially or in terms of job availability, sickness rates fall: conversely when jobs are secure and welfare benefits high, absenteeism tends to increase.

In terms of our present major health problems, the corollary of this individual decision-taking responsibility relates to the prevention or early diagnosis of common possibly life-taking conditions, like coronary heart disease (CHD) or some cancers. For instance, if someone goes for cancer screening or a coronary risk check, this decision implies that they are facing the possibility that they might have early cancer or pre-symptomatic coronary risk factors. They are, even if it is in response to social pressure, making a personal decision about their health.

What this book sets out to show is that, in today's state of medical and social development, personal decisions (based on understanding the forces and determinants of health) can play a major role in settling the balance, or loading the dice, between wellness and illness. Indeed, even where the sufferer is afflicted with some of the conditions just mentioned, personal attitudes can often make the difference between possible early death or normal life expectancy. Consequently, it is important for managers to understand these factors as well,

9

not only for the sake of their own health, but also in order to understand and possibly limit the pressures that confront their employees. Putting this into a wider perspective, we will look at concepts of health and disease under the following three headings:

- national and medical
- international
- personal.

NATIONAL AND MEDICAL ATTITUDES

Doctors and, to a considerable degree, their supporting cast (nurses, technicians, social workers, etc.) are all professionals trained in the national tradition of thinking about their problems, practising their skills and deploying available resources. Like all professionals, lawyers, accountants, theologians and some scientists, they qualify with a code of practice and set of beliefs about their 'art' which tends to be immutable and to last their lifetime.

- Professionals often take the line that it is only *they* that know what is good for *you*.
- Complacent acceptance of this tends to put them on a pedestal and to entrench their attitudes (they do, of course, enjoy playing God!).
- Doctors' beliefs and concepts about disease and methods of treatment are a reflection of their training and of the priorities and resources of the health service which the public wants and is prepared to pay for.

Obviously the way in which doctors operate and the arguments they put forward for resources and services to be provided,

11

must influence the thinking of the consumers in the society they serve. It is always difficult for a lay person, or even a politician, to argue with an expert. Consequently, the overall system for the management of health continues unchanged.

In an article published in *The Times* towards the end of 1989, comment was made about a survey of patient care carried out by the Consumers Association. The survey reflected a good deal of criticism about the relationship between doctors and patients, and the treatment prescribed, and concluded that there was often a communication gap between patients and General Practitioners.

Not all doctors accepted these conclusions, of course, although one based his criticism on the fact that the survey had been conducted among people who were well rather than those who were ill. Others, by implication, did accept the conclusions and the article referred to a doctor who had written to *The Physician* observing that:

> While general practice was evolving and must change if it were to survive, he felt that the appalling rigours of a medical education, coupled with the high academic standard demanded for entry into medical schools, produced a very well-qualified clinician who, although an articulate businessman, was socially inept, and found problems in communicating with his patients. As a result, there was no small talk in a consultation, and conversation was limited to medical detail, so that even the patient's nervous little joke, which might have led to an important revelation, was stifled by the look from an eye taught only to recognise biochemical data, not to communicate.

Traditionally, doctors are disease-oriented. Their training is based on their understanding and evaluation of both symptoms (calls for help) and overt physical changes, reinforced by a growing range of diagnostic procedures by which they can literally visualise the inside of all the body. In addition, they get increasing access to an expanding battery of powerful drugs and dramatic operative procedures. The result is the growing demand for an increasingly expensive range of cures, when better management might be to spend more time on the significantly less expensive area of prevention.

The point is that the service offered by the medical profession is based on its historical concept of illness and its possible cure. Being disease-oriented, doctors tend to regard symptoms as largely physically-based. Their priorities about the significance of individual diseases and methods of treatment are based on a series of beliefs which, of course, they have helped to create.

However, there are signs of change. Since the inception of the National Health Service in 1947, the medical and social services have been largely paid for out of taxes and not directly by the consumer at the point of consumption. Thus the elected government has allocated the resources but now, increasingly, the consuming public is wanting a say in determining the allocation of these resources, as to both overall funding and individual services.

To a certain extent, we are at a crossroads. Doctors (like other groups who have a monopoly over some form of public service, e.g. lawyers) are being increasingly told that the public must have the facility to make a choice. There is a growing awareness that the reason 'it's always been done this way and therefore it's the best way' is not necessarily acceptable. Consumers are beginning to tell doctors what they want from them, rather than doctors merely supplying what they believe is best for the consumer. Consequently, doctors are beginning to accept the challenge of being questioned rather than laying down their traditional law. Also, they are having to become more wellness-oriented and to face the fact that alternative therapies often have as much to offer (with perhaps less danger) than some of their traditional ones. The implications are that it is vital that we, the consumers, understand how to get our priorities right, and these must include the promotion of wellness as well as the treatment of disease.

INTERNATIONAL AND CROSS-CULTURAL ATTITUDES

If you were unlucky enough to have the same significant medical symptoms in New York, Paris and Frankfurt, you would soon discover that they were differently interpreted with even possibly different treatments being offered. This would be because the attitudes, priorities and training of the doctors in these cultures are different enough to provide differences in medical priorities and approaches to the patients' symptoms. Consequently, the interplay between medical tradition and consumer expectation in any one country is likely to produce different attitudes to health, disease and therapies. In America, for example, the whole approach to medicine is quite different.

- American medicine is a 'buyers' market with strong competition for patients who are, themselves, both critical and demanding.
- Patients expect to be offered the options for drugs and surgery and doctors have to make their case.
- Americans are health-conscious, prone to fashions in treatment and diet, etc. (but they have, over the last 10–15 years managed, by altering their lifestyle, to reduce significantly the incidence of heart disease).
- Medical behaviour in America, apart from being expensive with an inadequate safety-net for the not so well-off, is strongly defensive because of the very real threat of litigation.
- Consequently, costs are raised by the (to our standards) horrendous cost of the insurance cover for the specialists, which tends to produce over-treatment and investigation for safety's sake.

Standards of medical care are as high in America, France and Germany as they are here, but the latter two countries, particularly, do have different approaches to common diseases and a different range of therapies. The Germans, for instance, are very heart-oriented while the French rather go for the liver.

14

The point is that there are significant cultural differences in the perception of disease, the promotion of well-being and expectations as to what treatment is appropriate. For us in Europe, these differences may become quite important with the expected mobility within the European Community in the next few years. No one of these medical behaviour patterns is necessarily better than the other, although morbidity or mortality rates do vary from country to country.

Looking further afield, the *British Medical Journal* reported, towards the end of 1989, that the Japanese now have the longest life expectancy in the world, brought about by a dramatic increase in longevity over the last twenty years. A Japanese boy born in 1986 can expect to live 75.2 years (compared to 71.9 in the UK) whereas a girl can look forward to 80.9 years (compared to 77.7 here). Over the last twenty years, Japanese life expectancy has risen by between 7.5 and 8 years and, having had lower life expectancy than Britain, they now have a higher one.

Clearly, there must be some reasons why people are living longer in Japan and the clue seems to be that there is a lesser incidence of heart disease and cancer. It appears to be nothing to do with health expenditure and numbers of trained medical staff – Japan appears to spend about the same *per capita* on health services as Britain and also has fewer doctors and nurses per head of the population. They do, however, appear to devote more resources to prevention and screening and they certainly appear to have a better diet with less salt, less fat and fewer preserved foods. However, the most significant feature could well be the increase in gross national product (which is now higher than Britain's) and the fact that this increased income has been more evenly distributed.

Against this is a background of attitudes towards work, culture and social relationships. There is certainly the suggestion that Japanese domestic and industrial life is structured in a way which makes for less stress, more commitment and considerable stability.

Obviously, British attitudes and services are not necessarily the best; there is nothing sacrosanct about any one culture. Looking at trends in several countries, however, it is clear that some changes are for the better, whereas other trends, like attitudes to diet, smoking, drugs, alcohol and a sedentary life, may be for the worse.

PERSONAL ATTITUDES

Our individual approach to medical treatment is in many ways a reflection of the social culture in which we live.

- We tend to be too frightened of and perhaps grateful to our doctors to argue with them or suggest alternatives. However, 'medicine' is a consumer industry, paid for by the consumers who perhaps are entitled to and need to be encouraged to, express a view about the sort of service they want.
- The NHS may to a considerable degree be cost-effective, but the service some people get from hospital out-patient departments and doctors' surgeries would not be tolerated in a shop. We have become over-conditioned to waiting too patiently for medical attention.
- This can also apply to a doctor's attitude when confronted with a patient's problems and anxieties. There is often an apparent lack of caring and an apparent unwillingness to discuss individual problems (possibly due to the number of people in the waiting room). There is also too much prescribing of drugs (some of them potentially harmful) and the issuing of sick certificates.

The object of this book is to make the point that if we are well-informed and understand the things that make us tick for better or for worse, we can very largely control our own medical destiny. It is the job of the medical professional to guide us towards better health through enhanced well-being, accepting as a prerequisite that orthodox or traditional medicine does not necessarily hold all the keys to survival. The medical profession has it in its power to change our attitudes and to make us more responsible for our own well-being.

THE CONCEPT OF HOLISM

How you feel – whether cheerful, downcast, ebullient or tired – is much more a reflection of mood or emotion than it is of your physical state. If an exciting or stimulating suggestion comes along, it is easy to change gear and snap cheerfully into a new activity even at the end of a long and tiring day. There has been a change of mood, and mood, or the symptoms we present to the outside world, is the final common pathway of a range of mental and physical pressures and conflicts inside us.

These symptoms may be mental, emotional or behaviour-related, but because of the 'respectability' of being physically rather than behaviourally ill, we tend to develop physical symptoms. Thus the child who does not want to go to school develops tummy cramps. This is important and is called the 'somatisation of symptoms', which means that the distress is expressed in physical terms, rather than emotional or behavioural terms ('soma' is Greek for body).

This behaviour of the patient is then often reinforced by the doctor's training which follows the tradition that everything is symptom-orientated. The treatment then becomes a matter of treating the symptoms without necessarily looking for the cause. This can even extend to cases where there are genuine physical symptoms which are the manifestation of illness. Doctors find a cause for the symptoms, perhaps a duodenal ulcer, and treat them by drugs or surgery. Modern drugs like Zantec or Tagamet will quickly relieve the symptoms of dyspepsia but may not touch the real cause of the ulcer. However, it is now dawning on doctors that *why* someone is diseased is just as important as what is wrong with them. It may still be necessary to remove the diseased part but it remains important to seek the cause as well.

- Disease or distress is often lifestyle related and in order to evaluate symptoms the whole person must be analysed. This is called 'whole person' medicine. It involves time, listening and counselling, rather than drugs and X-rays.
- It does not necessarily or entirely involve doctors.

Anyone who is prepared to be a good, analytical and not necessarily too sympathetic a listener, can be a counsellor. There is enormous relief to be gained from sharing a problem – the sympathetic ear and the comforting shoulder.

- People with symptoms and anxieties quite reasonably want to be helped to feel better and increasing numbers of alternative and complementary therapies bear witness to the benefits of many of these systems offered by trained and experienced practitioners.

Homeopathy which listens before it prescribes, relaxation which relieves tensions, massage which is soothing, a diet which alters lifestyle, and so on, can all be better than an eight-minute consultation and a prescription from a general practitioner. Looking at the whole person and analysing their personal and inter-personal lifestyle, and not necessarily being therapeutically limited by orthodox medicine, is called 'holism' and the holistic approach is appreciated by growing numbers of people.

Public interest and the growing availability of complementary therapies is encouraging doctors to take a more holistic approach to their work. There are holistic centres and practices where doctors and the practitioners of complementary therapies work beneficially together for the benefit of their patients, who have access to a wider range of therapies.

SUMMARY

- Being ill arouses sympathy. Because doctors can help and because symptoms and solutions are outside most people's understanding, doctors are well respected in society.
- The solutions proposed are a factor of the training the

doctor has received and our expectations of the treatment to be given – often backed up by our uncritical acceptance of the doctor's recommendations. Both concepts reinforce one another – the doctor gives us what he or she thinks we want and we get what we think we ought to receive.

- Most of us conceive of illness in terms of physical symptoms but there is a growing body of opinion that does not accept that medicine can be compartmentalised in this way. The view is growing that, in many ways, illness is a reflection of the state of the *whole* body.

- It is therefore possible that the way we think, feel and act is as important to determine the causes of the illness as treating the symptoms of the illness. The way we think, feel and act could even have an impact on our susceptibility to illness.

This book is largely intended to help you understand the options available and to manage the health of yourself, your family and your staff. It is not intended to turn everybody into amateur doctors and it is certainly not intended to turn you into a hypochondriac, rushing to your medical dictionary every time you feel a twinge. It is, however, designed to teach you the basic concepts of wellness and it just might show you how to become a better spouse, a better parent, and a better boss.

CHAPTER TWO

HEALTH, LIFESTYLE AND WELL-BEING ————

INTRODUCTION

Because 'health' is as much a mental as a physical state it has, so far, defied precise definition in spite of many attempts. Doctors, from their disease-oriented base, tend to think of health in terms of the absence of disease: if you feel OK and don't complain of anything, you must be well. But the acceptance of the importance of the interaction between the body and the mind (called the 'psychosomatic' approach), followed more recently by the consolidation of this concept into holism, has helped to confirm a view held by many people, that health is a positive state of well-being and not merely the absence of disease or symptoms. People may drift through an unhappy life without being overtly ill but neither are they, in the holistic view, 'well'.

After the last war when the state of health in many countries was poor, the World Health Organisation defined health as being 'a state of physical, mental and social well-being'. This is a good working definition because it relates the individual to his or her physical, emotional and social environment. It implies that to be 'well', each of us must be reasonably in tune with these main aspects of our lives.

When the lifestyle-related assessment for a comprehensive

health check was being developed at the BUPA Medical Centre, the personality inventory was made under the headings of work, home and leisure (because although the doctors' experience was work-oriented and mostly paid for by employers, they discovered that as much stress came from home as from work).

Today, it would probably be more helpful to add 'involvement' to leisure. The professional often finds it difficult to separate work from leisure; in which category, for instance, would you put a business dinner or reading professional journals? Also the one-track workaholic who tends to have no leisure is both boring and vulnerable; activity outside work is essential to well-being and community involvement in particular is both contributing to society and widens relationships. The key word is 'balance', and the overall approach means that to remain in tune and balance with our environment in relation to our personal aspirations and attributes, is to be healthy.

This approach leads to two assumptions. The first is that any 'call for help' will be a response to conflict between, on the one hand, the individual and, on the other hand, their personality and the environment in which they live. The second assumption is that the most important part of treatment is to relieve symptoms, by removing or understanding the causes, rather than simply suppress them (which modern medicine tends to concentrate on). Clearly, to do this, the source of the conflict must be identified, which means that *why* someone is distressed or diseased is just as important as *what* (in traditional medical terms) is wrong with them. That, of course, doesn't deny any possible short-term benefit in the use of orthodox medical or surgical treatment, particularly for acute illness.

All this is clearly a simplification of a complicated series of inter-reactions between individuals and their environment. Nevertheless, the growing view is that the maintenance of health consists of balancing your underlying personality against the choices you can make about your environment, in order to work out the best deal for yourself. You won't win all the time but it is a prudent practice if you are to avoid severe defeat.

CHALLENGE AND STRESS

It is often useful to remember that, although humans have developed considerable skills at manipulating their physical environment, we are in biological terms very much part of a spectrum of living things, from the simplest single-celled organism, through plants and animals, to apes, with humans at the top of the evolutionary tree. It is likely, therefore, that there may be shared problems and common solutions.

Each living thing, in order to survive, has to overcome challenge and compete successfully with its environment, with its kith and kin and with other species. Failure means extinction whereas success means both an increase in numbers and evolutionary development. Overcoming challenge is an essential motivation to living and development and this is just as true for humans as for other forms of life; our lives are motivated by the need to overcome the challenges of daily living. Total sensory deprivation produces disorganisation of the personality: we actually need a steady stream of sensory input from outside to keep us stimulated and going. Dealing with challenge successfully produces the joys and satisfactions of life and is responsible for well-being. It is usually unrewarding to be unresponsive. For most of the developed countries, the most critical challenges are mainly social rather than physical. Food, warmth, water and shelter are, as it were, laid on.

Clearly, however, there must be times and occasions when the challenge wins and the individual or the species is defeated. Defeat can range from the trivial to the overwhelming, but it is part of living and if life is to go on there must be an equally fundamental defence mechanism against too much challenge. We must always be able to 'get off the hook' and give in gracefully.

When, particularly in human terms, challenge becomes too much and the escape routes are closed off, the balance is unsettled and we consequently become stressed. The term 'stress' was borrowed from engineering where, loosely, it means the capacity to withstand a measurable degree of strain, i.e. there is a threshold before distraction or stress sets in. The same is true for human reactions and, equally similarly, we can become 'pre-stressed' and raise our thresholds by training, experience and understanding.

Over recent years, 'stress' has become an in-phrase and indeed it has become almost fashionable to be under stress. However, the popularity of stress and being stressed has led to the phrase being loosely used and consequently confused with challenge, in terms of how it is understood by many people. In its true sense, becoming stressed is a reflection of a potential inability to cope with a set of challenges. People who are successfully carrying a heavy load may be tired but are not necessarily stressed. Their morale should be, and usually is, high because they are succeeding. Stress, and the reactions it provokes, on the other hand, is a manifestation of failure to cope: the moment when people must drop their load, yet are not permitted to do so, they become stressed. Stress occurs when there is no choice available, no obvious way out.

THE BIOLOGICAL IMPACT OF STRESS

Most of us take our bodies for granted and seldom stop to think about either how the main systems work or how they are integrated and controlled. Historically, for instance, it took a long time for people to accept that the blood actually circulated under pressure, and few understood what happened to the air that obviously went in and out of the lungs. The purpose of the brain and nervous system remained a mystery for much longer. Over the last hundred years, however, extensive and successful research has unravelled many of the secrets, not only of what individual organs and systems do but, even more important, how they are co-ordinated and controlled. It has become obvious that all living things (even the simplest organisms) must have some sort of control

24

system to obtain energy from food substances, reproduce, develop their embryo from a single cell to become an adult and then 'live successfully in a hostile environment.

In recent years, there has been considerable research into the functioning of individual cells and their covering or lining membrane. This has provided a much more precise understanding of how essential substances within the body are produced, how a message from the brain becomes an arm or a finger movement and how an outside stimulus, like pain, is received, transmitted and registered. We are, in fact, made up of a series of specialised cells, most of which have a single function. These are grouped into systems responsible for circulating the blood, moving the body, converting food into usable energy and storing any extra for later use, and so on. Clearly, all this activity has to be co-ordinated to function harmoniously for the body's good and, because nothing is static, there has to be an over-ride system to meet the needs of activity or adversity. There has also to be a maintenance service for repair and renewal and (earlier in life) for growth.

THE NEED FOR BALANCE

In the nineteenth century, when the outlines of these functions were being revealed, a famous French physiologist realised that in order to function correctly the internal environment had to be kept within very narrow limits. Consequently, many of the body's mechanisms are directed towards keeping the system stable or bringing it back to its centre point. It is all very like a sophisticated self-regulating servo-control system, i.e. the body works hard to maintain an overall balance.

A simple example will help to demonstrate all this. If physical activity is required, extra energy has to be provided. This, in turn, means more oxygen is needed, through an increased blood supply, faster breathing, and so on. Some of this activity produces biochemical changes which have to be counteracted to prevent a build up of excess alkali or acid, to which the body is sensitive.

Sugar is a relatively easily absorbed form of energy which goes into the bloodstream as glucose. More than a certain level of glucose is dangerous and may cause coma, as in diabetes, so blood sugar levels must be controlled. This is done by the production of a hormone (insulin – from cells in the pancreas) which controls blood sugar levels and facilitates the use of the glucose.

The successful regulation of body systems clearly involves very sophisticated functions and very sophisticated feedback, but the main point is that the more complex the systems and their controls, the easier it is for them to be disorganised and put out of service. Just as a simple fault will upset a computer and hence the systems it controls, so will major malfunctioning possibly produce a serious body disorder involving other systems.

TYPES OF SYMPTOMS

Our initial understanding of the functions and malfunctioning of the body's systems was necessarily based on the ability to see and measure physical change, which in turn related to physical symptoms like pain, indigestion, bleeding, skin rashes and so on. It was relatively easy to measure blood sugar, look at and count blood cells, X-ray the stomach and lung, etc., and so the history of medicine became based on the recognition of physical symptoms. There were also several forms of disturbed behaviour – madness – which had no obvious physical cause but were obviously 'there'. These were called psychoses and were dealt with by psychiatrists and the sufferers were largely isolated in an asylum.

Overall, symptoms and diseases were conveniently divided into two groups; organic (with changes that could be demonstrated and, it was hoped, dealt with, like removing a large stomach ulcer or treating diabetes with insulin); or psychotic (for the mentally deranged). Any rather vague symptoms, like abdominal or muscle pain, headache and anxiety, for which no changes could be identified, were called functional or neurotic and medicine had little to offer except for tender loving care in the physiotherapy department. It was only from the 1950s onwards that it gradually dawned on people that mental states involving anxiety could and did produce organic symptoms, and it also became clear that these mental states were quite capable of being responsible for what was previously thought to be physical change, like peptic ulcers or skin reactions.

All this may seem a long way from our starting point of challenge and stress, but in order to begin to understand how the body reacts to adversity, we need to have a very general outline of the principles on which the body functions. The main message here is that it functions as a very finely co-ordinated whole in which the mind and body – the mental and physical components – are inter-related. In very simple terms, if you fall over there may well be a bruise on your body (i.e. a physical symptom) but if you go through a bad patch at work, worry sets in, your mind becomes 'bruised', resulting in either physical or behavioural dis-ease, i.e. symptoms.

THE REACTIONS OF THE SUFFERER

The next and vital step in understanding stress is to realise that, because of the way in which it is constructed and integrated, the body cannot avoid reacting as a whole. Thus the underlying condition to which it is reacting can be either organic, physical, or mental.

In terms of looking for the causes of symptoms, it is important to remember that the body reacts as a whole and that the resulting symptoms can be physical or behavioural. What this means is that all symptoms are a call for help and are genuine and real to the sufferer.

The corollary of this is equally important. Just as we cannot divide our bodies up into convenient isolated chunks when trying to identify the cause of symptoms, neither can we divide our lives up in the same way. We like to think that we can cleverly chop ourselves up into functional slices, taking half to work and leaving the rest at home, but a look back at one's problems shows that worry about, say, job security or a sick child, can feed back into the way we behave at home or in the office. Thus our overall well-being is a reflection of what the whole of our life – work, home and leisure – is doing to us. Analysing the causes of our symptoms should start with an analysis of our lifestyle.

A popular truism is that we are all unique. We start by being the product of our genes which give us a mixture of strengths and weaknesses. These factors are then honed by our experience of living, learning and relating. All our experiences determine our personality and how it reacts to the environment. Extroverts react differently from introverts; the anxious to the placid; the leader to the led – and so on. As challenge is essential to satisfy motivation, the trick of survival is to be objective enough to keep our attributes and aspirations more or less in balance. Get the challenges out of balance and stress will be along to even things out.

The final point to be made here, in this over-simplified account of a complex situation, is that, although they exist, nearly all these reactions are both unconscious and automatic. We are aware of the symptoms – the calls for help – but we seldom know what the calls are about or where they come from. When life got too much, the Victorians got the vapours; we might get pre-menstrual tension or migraine. Both are a reaction to get us off a hook or out of a conflict.

No one is good at everything and we all have our breaking points and are vulnerable in some direction or another. However, success in one sphere boosts morale and provides reserves of satisfaction to deal with other problems. Which is why one-track workaholics are so vulnerable, particularly as they get older, as all their eggs are in the work basket. Relax and enjoy life.

THE BALANCE OF WELLNESS

Humankind's physical, biological and mental evolution (which is still continuing) has given us a relatively smoothly functioning body which is remarkably successful in maintaining its status quo in the face of all manner of problems. Nevertheless, with an apparatus as complicated as this, a lot of things can and do go wrong and cause illness, much of which modern medicine can deal with. It is really only in about the last hundred years that medical treatment has made significant contributions to survival (clean water, better hygiene, housing, food and education have done more for mass survival than drugs or surgery). Before this, accepted treatment was based on hope and expectation, and was often downright dangerous with its draughts, cuppings and purgings. But because of the way in which medical practice was structured and the ways in which its problems were seen, all attention was, and largely still is, focused on the sufferer. However, the more important and often unanswered question is – why are some people never ill?

It has been legitimate for many years to talk about resistance to disease. Indeed, resistance to infections that produce immunity, like polio-myelitis, tuberculosis or smallpox, can be measured in the blood. We also know that parts of our so-called immune system, our general resistance, is affected by attitude and emotion. There is also a growing volume of documented experience in relation to cancer cures, in which something emotional or physical which alters lifestyle appears to raise resistance or at least holds the cancer at bay. Because of the relationship between mood, body tone and resistance, it is claimed that attitudes and happiness make for well-being and promote wellness. This leads to the suggestion that within us, as part of our intricate and sophisticated balancing controls, there must be an overall balance that tips us in one way or another. How we actually are and feel must be the final common pathway of all the inputs and outcomes of trying to live.

SUMMARY

- Health is well-being and can be defined as a well-balanced lifestyle where our basic attributes equate satisfactorily with the way we decide to live.
- Challenge is an essential motivation to living but inability to cope with challenge produces stress. An unbalanced lifestyle (where we cannot cope with the challenge of what we would like to be) will produce stress.
- The body is a finely-balanced mechanism and it can be unbalanced by stress. The symptoms, however, may be physical and not necessarily mental.
- If we keep our lifestyle in balance we will have a better chance of keeping our bodies in balance, i.e. we may remain healthy and not become unwell.

Happy, well-adjusted people facing the right challenges don't appear to have the time to be ill. They are the survivors. How to be in this class and put your children on at least the right starting line is what the rest of this book is about: we all have the option of managing our own health.

CHAPTER THREE

ASSESSING THE RISK —————

INTRODUCTION

You can look at optimising your chances of being healthy as a management problem. The management of any enterprise consists of running the enterprise in such a way that you maximise the chances of meeting the objectives. This in turn implies the following:

- Getting the best available information about the environment in which you intend to operate your business and to have defined objectives for it.
- Having a thorough understanding of the risks involved.
- Running the business in a way which minimises the risks.
- Constructing a management control system against which to monitor progress.

Some of the satisfaction of management comes, of course, from taking calculated risks, though it is also wise to know when to cut your losses and to resist the temptation to throw good money after bad. Getting out in good time is better than being sent to the receiver. A valuable help in management can be the proper use of expert advisers with a good course record, although one of the skills of management is to know when to back your own judgement and disregard advice. Two trends now make it possible to think of individual health promotion in much the same general terms, i.e. as a personal management problem.

- The first is that a well-balanced approach to life is a major determinant of well-being and very much under individual control.
- The second is that there is now a considerable amount of hard evidence about the incidence and causes of the main 'killer diseases'. There is a pay-off in taking avoiding action by living more prudently, i.e. by avoiding unnecessary risks.

It is also sensible to look at health management as a family, group or social problem, as well as an individual one. For example, if the overall instance in Britain of coronary heart disease (CHD) is to be reduced to the levels in other developed countries, our national eating habits, as well as some other habits, will have to be considerably altered. Before setting out some of the management information on health, two provisos have to be made.

- All statistics are averages and therefore they cannot necessarily be applied to all individuals. The fact that people with a raised level of certain blood fats have, say, three times the coronary risk, does not mean either that all those in the high-level group will be afflicted or that all those in the low-level group will survive.
- The main point of this book is in getting people to adjust their behaviour in order to reach retirement sound enough in mind and limb to enjoy their later years, and not either to die prematurely or be burnt-out wrecks. It is not a specialist book designed to turn you into a long-distance runner or to help you lose weight.

Another factor here may be that the decline in the number of younger people coming into employment will have two effects on the workforce. The first is that everybody will be able, if they so want, to work for longer, and the second is that there will be, inevitably, a much wider role for women in commerce and industry. A separate chapter is given on their particular problems, which as will be seen, need to be understood by their male colleagues. The information required for health management can be listed under a number of headings, as follows:

- The incidence of the principle diseases.
- Risk factors relating to the individual, i.e. genetic make-up, sex, and personality.
- Behavioural risk factors like diet, lifestyle, smoking, exercise, and relationships, etc.
- Social, environmental and geographical factors.
- The cause of the most prevalent disease, i.e. cardio-vascular disease.

THE INCIDENCE OF MAJOR DISEASES

Life expectancy can be expressed in two ways. The first is from birth, which includes the hazards of early life and will obviously lower the overall or average life expectancy. The second is life expectancy from mid-life onwards, i.e. if you get this far safely, you can expect to go further and live for longer. Both expectancies have increased over the past two decades and the fact that more people are living well into their 80s and even 90s is producing new individual and social problems. Few very elderly people will be able to cope on their own and about 20 per cent will be mentally confused.

Table 1 shows, in simplified form, the main causes of deaths at all ages for men and women. It also illustrates the changes in these between 1951 and 1987.

Table 2 gives a more detailed picture in relation to causes of death in terms of sex and age. It shows that heart disease and strokes are far more prevalent in middle-aged men than women. This makes CHD for middle-aged men a major medical and personal problem: the incidence rose steadily since the last world war and is only now levelling off and

Table 1 Main causes of death for males and females, 1951 and 1987

Table 2 Most common causes of death, 1984 (totals in brackets)

Age	Men			Women		
25-34	accidents (875)	cancer (507)	suicide (484)	cancer (619)	accidents (185)	suicide (128)
35-44	cancer (1,359)	heart disease (1,332)	accidents (690)	cancer (1,992)	stroke (229)	suicide (211)
45-64	heart disease (24,472)	cancer (20,098)	stroke (3,628)	cancer (17,806)	heart disease (7,074)	stroke (2,823)
65+	heart disease (62,898)	cancer (51,168)	stroke (23,108)	heart disease (61,265)	cancer (45,575)	stroke (41,136)

Source: HMSO Social Trends

beginning to fall. Sadly, Britain is still higher up the international coronary league than the rest of Europe.

Most of us have a fear of dying painfully of cancer, and perhaps because of this are often reluctant to take early symptoms to the doctor. Also, lay people often think of cancer as a single condition but, in fact, it is a large family of tumours with different patterns in regard to the cells involved, the sex and age of the individual, and to the role or function of the cells. Table 3 shows the relative incidence of cancers in men and women. Lung cancer is still the commonest in men and has virtually now approached the same incidence in women as breast cancer. The incidence of coronary thrombosis in women is increasing also, probably due to the gradual change in overall lifestyle as their role in industry and commerce changes.

Table 3 Numbers of cancer deaths, 1984 (all ages)

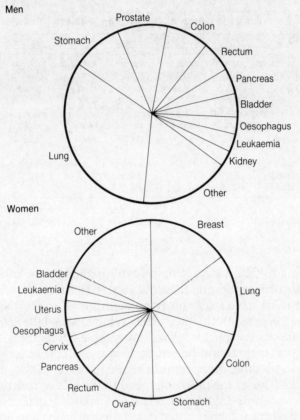

Source: OPCS Monitor DH2

INDIVIDUAL FACTORS WHICH AFFECT SUSCEPTABILITY TO DISEASE

We have already seen that there are differences in the risk factors for various diseases between men and women. Women, of course, have a range of conditions that they are uniquely susceptible to. These are dealt with in more detail in Chapter 7.

Genetic factors

Within the nucleus of every cell is the genetic material which controls cell function and which, right at the start of life, determines the sex and other major attributes of the new individual and his or her constituent parts. The discovery of DNA (the 'double helix') was an exciting breakthrough in understanding the control systems and the role played by individual genes. Genes control the formation of cells, and genes are inherited; inheritance, therefore, clearly plays a large part in determining who we are and how we function. Consequently, some malfunctioning which causes disease is either inherited or based on developed gene malfunction.

It is known, for example, that there is a direct relationship between certain blood fats and CHD. The lack of a certain gene determines the absence of a related enzyme to deal with this particular form of fat, which then piles up in the blood, is absorbed by the artery wall and finally blocks the artery causing tissue damage and possible early death.

Now that genes can be individually identified and manipulated, the whole growing field of genetic engineering offers untold possibilities for altering or improving gene behaviour. In a way related to this new knowledge, is an understanding of how our protective or immune system functions at a cellular level, important because allergies and sensitivities, as well as the inability to deal with infections and noxious substances, are a common cause of dis-ease.

Coronary vulnerability is quite often inherited, particularly through the mother, and passed on to males. Additionally, a few cancers are genetically determined so screening of vulnerable people should be started early and continued through life. With prior warning, many inheritable conditions can be picked up at or before birth and appropriate action taken. Increasingly, too, if there is a known genetic risk, specific counselling is available about the risks and possible mitigation.

The main point about genetic tendencies is that, although you can do nothing about them, you can avoid taking other risks over which you do have control. If you know there is a tendency to CHD in your family you should certainly think even more carefully before, for example, taking up smoking.

Personality and mood

Meyer and Friedman, two American heart specialists, described the go-getting, manic, target-oriented executive as a type A personality, who is coronary prone and has the following characteristics:

- easily irritated
- feels guilty when relaxing
- shows impatience with people
- takes on excessive responsibilities
- trys to master uncontrollable situations
- gets upset when things go wrong
- has difficulty in confiding in people
- has trouble solving family problems
- has severe sense of time urgency
- tries to work on two or more projects at once
- neglects all aspects of personal life in favour of work
- sacrifices leisure time
- eats, moves and works rapidly
- talks fast and explosively.

They were, unfortunately, of the opinion that persuading such people to calm down was not generally possible until they had suffered their first coronary. At that point (provided they survived and learnt) they became a better person and lived rather than existed, thereby reducing their chances of getting a further coronary.

Anxious, tense, manic and highly-strung ambitious people are usually 'uptight'. Their blood pressure tends to be high, they are often screwed up inside, bad at managing relationships, and over-tired. They don't take holidays, can't relax or switch off and it is not surprising that they are coronary-prone. They are out of balance and tend to reach middle-age without much steam left in their boilers or any interests outside work.

We will come back to stress under self-management and coping skills, but the point to realise now is that the risk factors are often personality, mood and lifestyle-related, and thus under individual control. They present each of us with a personal management problem.

Today, in every area of our society, there is a real risk of mental ill-health. We should be on the look-out for it, be prepared to consider it as any other disease, and find a sensible doctor who will treat it honestly. Clearly, if there is a genetic or family disposition to mental ill-health, it is worth getting further advice about. Mood, which is often the critical factor in mental equilibrium, is naturally a reflection of basic personality and experience. Some of us are made of stronger stuff than others, but the fussers, the worriers and the obsessionals are at more risk because they tend to eat themselves up with tension and anxiety. They should be honest enough to, and their friends and families should press them to, seek advice and perhaps learn to relax. Not knowing yourself and failing to seek advice is a risk factor.

The cholesterol story

A survey in America in the 1950s, in which everyone in a township was screened and then followed up over many years, brought to light a number of facts about cholesterol:

- Men with raised cholesterol levels, many of whom were obese, had a higher coronary risk.
- Smokers with raised cholesterol levels had an even higher risk.
- Not all high cholesterol people were necessarily vulnerable, and people with more or less normal levels were not necessarily safe.
- Cholesterol in the blood was a complex package of lipo-proteins (fats of various sorts). These fell into two main groups in relation to their molecular size, the high and low density lipo-proteins.
- It turned out to be the low density lipo-proteins (LDL) that were dangerous and got deposited in the blood vessel lining. The high density (HDL) molecules were beneficial and mostly used by the body for energy.

How an individual deals with dietary fats depends on a number of things, but two key factors are the type of fat being eaten and the genetic inheritance of the eater, in terms of body build and metabolic efficiency in dealing with dietary fats (i.e. the obese store fat but hyperactive, thin ectomorphs burn up their energy). LDL is largely to be found in saturated animal and dairy fats with HDL turning up in unsaturated vegetable oil fats. In dietary terms a lot more is known about various individual fatty acids and fat components. For example, at the time of writing herring oil is generally regarded as being protective.

Another important factor is the proportion of total dietary energy that comes from fat. The Japanese, who have a lower coronary rate than the British, not only get half as much of their energy from fat but most of this is unsaturated, non-animal fat. Other information has also emerged, like the fact that exercise increased the good HDL factor and smoking the bad LDL factor. Personality comes into this, too, because, through the workings of the internal psychosomatic control system, the stressed type A personality, common in managers, has raised cholesterol levels largely made up of LDL.

Women go through hormonal change at the menopause which causes their cholesterol levels to rise, and it may be because of this that they get their coronaries twenty years later than men. Altering hormonal balance appears to have an influence on the coronary rate, and hormone replacement therapy (HRT), which postpones the menopause and delays the cholesterol rise, may have other benefits but there are always disadvantages in manipulating hormones over too long a period. This is discussed further in Chapter 7.

Finally the good news, at least for those who enjoy a drink, is that alcohol taken in moderation (particularly wine apparently), puts up HDL. This may contribute to the mystery of why the French and Italians have such a low coronary rate, though the French particularly do have a high incidence of liver damage from alcohol.

BEHAVIOURAL FACTORS WHICH AFFECT SUSCEPTABILITY TO DISEASE

Eating habits

The digestive system, when it works well, is a flexible but superbly integrated system for taking in a wide range of foods and breaking them down into their constituent parts. These are then absorbed into the body and used, stored, or reconstructed into other substances; what is not wanted is then got rid of. A good analogy is to think of a model house built from Lego. This can be taken to pieces and all or some of the separate blocks used to build a totally different structure. It used to be thought that quantities of fats, carbohydrates and proteins were the main food requirements. However, these are much more interchangeable by the body and its metabolic system than was thought, and there is, in fact, a relatively small range of absolutely essential substances that have to be available. These include amino acids, vitamins, and minerals like iron and calcium.

This digestive flexibility makes possible the vast and changing array of diets for better health, weight control, or simply variety. When, however, the digestive system gets out of kilter for internal or external reasons, the situation gets quite complicated because of a whole range of diseases or upsets.

It is also very sensitive to the emotions, with highly-strung people often having delicate digestive systems. Perhaps because of this, the digestive system seems responsive to suggestion and may react unfavourably to certain substances. This may take the form of a failure to absorb, or of sensitivity or allergy, but this is too wide a field to explore in further detail here. It also has to adjust to the dietary fashions adopted by its owner. But lucky are the ones who live at peace with their digestive systems!

Obesity

Obesity is described as a disease because, during the 1940s, the American life insurance companies got together, pooled their mortality data and found that obese people had a significantly increased mortality largely due to hypertension. Mortality apart, obesity leads to increased vulnerability to conditions such as diabetes, limits mobility and puts a growing strain on an ageing frame and joints. Since then, with much more knowledge about risk factors and the natural history of hypertension, the general feeling now is that moderate obesity is probably less dangerous than was originally thought. If, however, there is even moderate high blood pressure in middle-age (45–64) it may well need to be controlled by weight loss – otherwise drugs will be required.

Defining obesity is surprisingly difficult as body build varies independently of fat content. Thus, heavily built, large boned and well-muscled mesomorphic people may be wrongly accused of being obese. Most insurance companies' weight tables are based on averages and for a long time Britain relied on American averages (although it soon became clear that there was a greater number of obese Americans than Europeans). Ten per cent over average weight is usually acceptable but anything over this probably requires action. Researchers into obesity now use a measurement called the 'body mass index', which is your weight in kilos, divided by your height in metres, and the resulting figure squared. Arbitrary cut-off points are taken, and an index of 25 is regarded as being on the plump side and 30 as obese. Table 4 shows that over a third of us are at least plump.

Most seriously obese people are aware that they present a bad image and it is said that inside them is a 'thinny' trying to get out. The very fat often have a personality disorder but most moderately obese folk have allowed themselves to develop poor eating habits, many of which started in child-hood.

Table 4 Percentage of population overweight
and obese, by sex, 1980

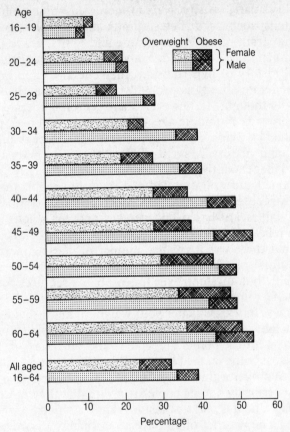

Source: OPCS Heights and Weights of Adults in Great Britain

Diet and nutrition

A clear distinction has to be made between diet and nutrition.

- Diet is the totality of what we eat. Clearly, it has to be basically nutritious and, it is hoped, enjoyable, but if there is a specific problem such as a failure to deal with carbohydrates (as in diabetes) a special diet is required.
- Nutrition is the study of what an individual or a species – plant, animal – minimally requires to maintain their body in growth, normal activity and repair.

It is possible to make the following overall observations about our eating behaviour:

- Some foods are more nutritious than others in terms of energy or essential components. Fibre, for instance, which is not absorbed, provides bulk (for effective digestion) but no calories.
- There is very little malnutrition in Britain, the main problem being quite the opposite, namely that too much is eaten. About 30 per cent of the population is over-weight, which is a moderately serious risk-factor in terms of hypertension, CHD, diabetes and reduced physical activity.
- We have become increasingly accustomed to eating too much of the wrong foods. This is largely in terms of animal fats and dairy products containing saturated fats, and also salt and sugar.
- Eating is very much a matter of habit, based on family and social group mores. A more sensible national diet is one of the reasons for the reduction of the CHD rate in the USA, Australia and Scandinavia.
- We need to eat less, avoid 'junk' foods, and concentrate more on natural, uncontaminated and fresh foods. The digestive system is based on the food being squeezed through the intestines, which means, particularly as one gets older and the system gets more sluggish, that there must be enough bulk in the diet to be squeezed through.
- So-called convenience foods lack bulk, hence the need for and the popularity of a high fibre diet, which has the additional virtue of being low calorie and cholesterol reducing.

The 'Green' movement has brought new interest in vegetarianism and, provided the right mixture of foods is taken, it is perfectly nutritious. There is some evidence that vegetarians live longer, possibly because of a lower incidence of CHD. This may be due to lack of animal fat in their diet and also because it is more difficult to eat enough vegetables, etc. to be seriously overweight. Extreme Vegan vegetarianism, however, can be dangerous because of folic acid deficiency (which can cause pernicious anaemia).

Cigarette smoking

- Nicotine is a tranquilliser and also a subtle addictive drug. Nicotine and alcohol probably cause more deaths and disability than the 'hard' drugs, but take longer to have these effects and are cheaper to buy and legally available.
- Smoking is now a minority activity, indulged in by about a third of the population.
- Inhaling tobacco smoke, which is the dangerous bit, causes lung cancer, chronic bronchitis and contributes significantly to coronary heart disease.
- Women (whose take-up of smoking has increased in the last forty years) now have an incidence of lung cancer equal to that of the breast. Also, smoking in pregnancy is positively harmful to the foetus. The CHD rate is increasing in women who smoke. Table 5 shows the incidence in lung cancer in both men and women in recent years.

  Note that the incidence of lung cancer in women has doubled since 1957. This is almost certainly the delayed effect of smoking. In men, the rate is beginning to come down as the results of men stopping smoking are coming through. But, as Table 1 showed, the incidence of respiratory disease which is smoking-related is still high and this is especially true in social classes 4 and 5.
- 'Passive smoking' (breathing in other people's exhaled smoke) has been shown to produce a slight, but significant

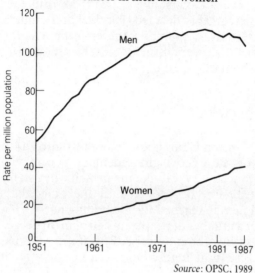

Table 5 Changing mortality rates from lung cancer in men and women

Source: OPSC, 1989

increase in lung cancer among non-smokers.
- Smoking raises blood pressure and pulse rate, liberates adrenaline (which releases sugar), raises LDL, and puts up blood carbon monoxide levels to about 16 per cent in those who have efficient lungs left. This is a far higher concentration than is allowed, for instance, at a work site.
- The adrenaline (sugar effect) is why people, when they stop smoking, get a craving for sugar. When stopping, it is sensible to deal with smoking first and, when stable, deal with any weight increase as a secondary problem.
- Carbon monoxide, apart from reducing the oxygen-carrying capacity of the blood, damages the lining of the arteries, thereby encouraging the deposition of cholesterol. Filter tips may remove a lot of the irritant tar, but they alter the temperature of combustion and increase the carbon monoxide level in the tobacco smoke. CHD

is statistically a more important reason than lung cancer for not smoking.

- Smokers are addicts, like alcoholics or drug takers, who have presumably decided that they don't mind shortening their lives, polluting the environment for others, and making it very difficult for their children to see why they shouldn't smoke too.

Lack of exercise

The late Winston Churchill is frequently cited as the prime example of the overweight sedentary person who found exercise unnecessary. Unlike the person who, on feeling the urge to exercise, lies down until the mood has passed, Churchill merely reached for the brandy bottle! There is no doubt that a number of people, not all of them obese, manage perfectly well without exercise. But, for most of us, regular physical activity is highly beneficial not only for its direct physiological benefits but also because it is a catalyst for feeling better, performing better, and because of the self discipline involved. It also helps you to sleep better.

It was the medical department of London Transport which showed that bus conductors had a lower CHD rate than the more sedentary servo-assisted drivers. Since then this finding has been reinforced by a lot more work, including a long-term survey of civil servants. Being sedentary is a risk factor.

Don't forget, all muscle has to be used if it is to retain its strength, and the heart muscle is no different. Regular physical activity helps the heart to withstand the onset of a thrombosis and seemingly reduces the risk of it happening in the first place. Even when the heart has been damaged by a coronary, or after a reparative by-pass operation, rehabilitation involves supervised physical activity to improve muscle performance.

Alcohol dependency

Alcohol dependency which, in many cases, arises from the easy availability of alcohol at home and at work, plus social pressure to associate alcohol with most social contact, must be regarded as a risk factor of increasing importance, particularly to the young. Alcohol dependency is a complicated hazard of life today and social mores play a large part in its development. Table 6 dramatically illustrates the increase in alcohol consumption, particularly in young people over the period. As it represents average *per capita* consumption, i.e. the drinkers and the non-drinkers, the *per capita* consumption of young drinkers must be appreciably higher. The growth in alcohol consumption must give cause for alarm.

The consumption of alcohol appears to be increasing as part of the 'better life'. Also, it is relatively cheap and, perhaps, far too easily available. We don't know much about why some people fail to mature as reasonably controlled social drinkers and either drink too much or become overtly alcohol dependent.

Alcohol is a subtle addictive drug which, in its middle stages of development, produces a tolerance in the drinker. Thus the dependent, unlike the smoker, tends to drink more to gain the same effect. When, later, the metabolic system (largely in the liver), breaks down, it takes even longer to metabolise alcohol so that the same amount may last longer and seemingly have a greater effect. Some people find, as they get older, that they can drink less to achieve the same effect as when they were younger. This is probably because their livers are less efficient but not necessarily seriously damaged.

Liver problems are not necessarily the sign of heavy drinking. They may also have a chemical or genetic basis, because some people lack the enzymes to cope with alcohol. Liver function tests (carried out as part of routine screening) show that many people had no problem because they found a little drink went a long way and drank hardly anything at all, whereas others damaged their livers with a small quantity of alcohol. The liver function test is a useful screening device because it tells the heavy regular business drinker that he or

Table 6 Average number of units of alcohol consumed weekly by age and sex, 1979 and 1987

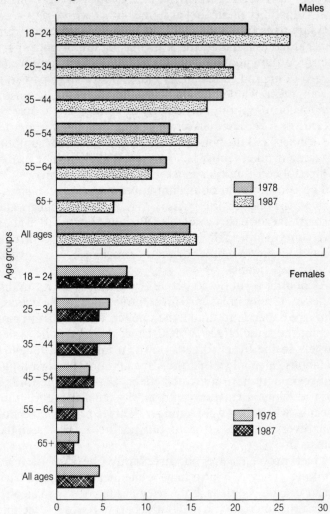

Source: OPCS, *Drinking in England and Wales in 1987*

she is consuming more than their liver can cope with.

Alcohol is rapidly absorbed, particularly on an empty stomach, and circulated all over the body. It is detoxicated by the liver but is also excreted in the breath and the urine. Blood alcohol levels are a more accurate measure of the true concentration than the level in the breath, or the breathalyser.

Chemically and addictively, it is ethyl alcohol that does the damage. What it is mixed with only gives the taste, i.e. wine, sherry, vermouth, gin, whisky, etc., but behaviourally it is the basic chemical that counts. Individuals do have preferential tolerances as to the form of alcohol they can either enjoy or be upset by, but this has nothing to do with the addiction to alcohol itself. A sudden intolerance, say, to red wine, is not uncommon and relates to substances in the drink to which the sensitivity develops.

The interesting thing about alcohol is that it has two quite different effects, on mood and the liver, and it is the mood alteration that we mostly enjoy. It works socially by depressing inhibitions and liberating mood, hence the rising decibel index at a cocktail party, but it surprises people to learn that, pharmacologically, alcohol is a depressant and was at one time used to deaden pain during operations. It is, however, a poor anaesthetic because the margin between coma and death is too narrow for safe surgery.

Increasing over-consumption of alcohol is now a major social problem and in personal and managerial terms, leaders, managers, etc., do have a responsibility in setting personal, social and business standards for consumption.

SOCIAL, ENVIRONMENTAL AND GEOGRAPHICAL FACTORS WHICH AFFECT SUSCEPTABILITY TO DISEASE

Factors like the work we do, where we live, our social class, urban and rural differences, and so on, do have an impact on our susceptibility to illness. It is, for instance, a sad fact that the incidence of coronary thrombosis is four times greater in social class 5 than in the professional classes. There are quite significant geographical differences too, both in the instance of respiratory disease and cancer. The availability of resources for treatment in different areas and parts of the country may also be significant.

Thus, where you live and what you do can be critical decisions although, of course, not everyone has a choice. Clearly, living next to a large chemical works, nuclear power station or motorway must carry higher risks than living in a country village. Equally, a long journey to work, three to four hours perhaps, or even one to two hours travel per day, is a major determinant of lifestyle. Professional people do, in fact, often have wider choices than they care to admit. They may also live longer and more happily if they were to contemplate changing gear in mid-life and stop running to stand still. Big fish live longer in small ponds.

THE CAUSE OF CARDIOVASCULAR DISEASE

The arteries are the blood vessels which carry oxygen-rich blood to the body. The coronary arteries in particular take blood to the heart muscle and are said to run round the heart like a crown, hence their name.

An artery is a muscular walled conduit with a delicate lining, and blood is circulated partly by the pumping action of the heart which expels blood into the arteries and stretches them and partly by the elastic rebound of the artery wall which helps to squeeze the blood through the system.

For a variety of reasons, particularly when damaged, the artery lining picks up cholesterol which is deposited in its wall where it builds up until blood can no longer circulate. It then clots and the muscle being supplied dies from lack of oxygen. This means that the seriousness of a coronary depends on the size of the artery involved and the extent of the blockage. Chronically blocked coronary arteries can be re-placed by vein grafts – the 'by-pass' operation which is now widely available. Often, too, they can be 'reamed out' by sophisticated devices passed down the artery or even by stretching. If these new processes fail, the by-pass operation is still available and can, indeed, be repeated more than once.

The elasticity of the cardio-vascular system is variable. If blood pressure rises (hypertension), the arteries tend to react by thickening and becoming rigid. If the arteries themselves become rigid (arteriosclerosis), the heart has to work harder to maintain an adequate circulation, i.e. blood pressure has to rise. Thus, alteration of either the heart or the arteries can promote hypertension.

Clearly, being a working machine, the less work the heart has to do, the longer it is likely to go on remaining efficient. This implies keeping blood pressure within normal limits. Blood pressure varies all the time with demand, activity and emotion. Anger and tension raise blood pressure; relaxation lowers it. The workload of the heart is also clearly related to body size and volume. Thus, obese people tend to have higher blood pressures and make more demands on their heart. If too great a load is placed on the heart, then it will finally give up the struggle and we suffer from heart failure.

High blood pressure also effects artery walls. With sustained hypertension there comes a time when the vessels may either block – as in the coronaries – or burst under pressure. This happens mostly in the brain and is called a stroke. With either a haemorrhage or a blockage, part of the brain is damaged and ceases to function, causing paralysis of the regions supplied.

The cardio-vascular circulatory system can therefore be considered in much the same way as a sophisticated central heating system, with sensors to maintain a predetermined set of conditions, except that the control is mainly over pressure, rather than temperature.

The risk factors

Coronary heart disease, of which we still experience a serious epidemic (see Table 7), is the best example of a significant and increasingly preventable disease from which a number of risk factors have been identified and which can then be modified with benefit to the individual and the group involved. It is now established that the changes or factors on page 55 seem to predispose to CHD and make a person coronary prone.

Table 7 Mortality rates from coronary artery disease by sex, 1951–87

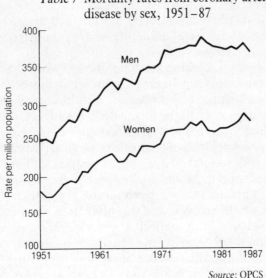

Source: OPCS

- genetic inheritance
- lack of exercise
- cigarette smoking
- obesity
- diet unrelated to obesity
- stress, tension and anxiety
- hormone balance, particularly in women
- minor factors like water hardness, mineral deficiency, etc.

RISK ASSESSMENT – THE MOT

We can look at health screening, or the properly done health check, as very much the same as having a car serviced. Regular car servicing is recommended by the manufacturers to stop the vehicle breaking down. Plant and machinery with moving parts have to be periodically inspected, if only for safety reasons. The same arguments can be applied to our human machinery; by regularly taking certain measurements we can monitor wear and tear, deal with symptoms and, as with coronary risk factors, pick up pre-symptomatic changes in blood pressure or blood chemistry before irreversible harm has occurred.

Clearly, nothing is perfect and because of human variation, the occasional person with normal indices will drop down dead. But most won't and if you are to manage your health you must know what the odds are. You do not and cannot know your blood pressure or cholesterol level until it is measured: you have to be mature to live with the results. It is surely more dangerous to run away from possible anxiety than to find out and deal with the problem at an early stage. Also, being reassured by normality is a perfectly legitimate benefit. There are two parts to a good health check:

- The first mechanical bit is the measuring of height, weight, blood pressure, X-ray (possibly), cardiograph, blood chemistry, and so on, followed by a full physical examination.
- Just as important is the lifestyle-related consultation. Before evaluating any symptoms or past diseases, a full personal and family history is taken, looking at work, home and leisure. The presence or absence of symptoms can then be related back to this history, and the 'why' of disease will be revealed.

Armed with the results of these two procedures, there could be a consultation session to discuss problems or just issue reassurance and encouragement – which is deserved and perfectly legitimate. The doctor can congratulate you on being well. It must also be remembered that the first check establishes a baseline against which future improvement or deterioration can usefully be charted.

From the management point of view, an experienced doctor, after having seen perhaps the ten or twenty more senior managers in a company, can get a fairly good idea of the health climate within that organisation. Advice can then be given not only to individuals about their personal problems but also to the organisation about the overall morale and motivation within the company.

Comparative company profiles can be prepared covering the various risk factors and stress. These can be very revealing and obviously relate to the tradition and activities within the firm.

Full health checks need not be complicated or expensive and they are rapidly becoming something that more and more people (and companies) want. Single disease checks, like for diabetes, breast and cervical cancer, glaucoma, deafness and vision defects in children, and so on, should also be encouraged and supported. Some companies, for instance, offer their staff a nationwide breast screening service. Work-site screening – to minimise time off work – will become much more common over the next few years.

Health maintenance is prudence, not hypochondria, and it starts with you not your doctor. Public demand could quickly make it part of a revitalised approach to the nation's health.

SUMMARY

- If health is a balanced lifestyle, it is important for the management of health to know the factors which can upset the balance.
- The key factors which affect us are inheritance, the way we behave and the environment in which we live.
- Each risk factor alone can be assessed, but multiple risk factors multiply the effect through a form of odious synergy: $2 + 2 = 5$.
- CHD is a major epidemic in the UK but many of the factors which cause it are within our control.
- Regular health checks are important (rather like keeping a medical 'log-book') as they will identify the risk factors and help us to monitor our well-being.

Assessing the risk factors is an important part of health management. Once we know what these factors are and how they work, we can then start devising a lifestyle which will take these risk factors into account and allow us to stack the odds more in our favour. This is what the next chapter deals with.

CHAPTER FOUR

PLANNING AND MANAGING YOUR LIFESTYLE ————

INTRODUCTION

So far, we have suggested that health and well-being are very much a function of a balanced lifestyle and consequently under personal control. We have also looked at some of the main hazards and pitfalls to be avoided, so now we can start to set out a framework of how we might manage our lifestyle. These choices come in two somewhat conflicting categories, first the personal and the professional, i.e. home and career, and second the physical and the emotional.

The options you choose are a balance between the ground rules of survival and your own aspirations and attributes. These latter should be seen as the design limitations on your performance, so objectivity in assessing your strengths and weaknesses and recognising the warning signs of stress is helpful. Consequently, the health check (the equivalent of an auditor's report) can be very beneficial; profit on turnover satisfactory: could do better: problems over marriage require investigation, etc. Another useful checkpoint is to look now and again into the metaphorical mirror and ask yourself two questions; 'What am I like to work for and with?', and 'What am I like to live with?'. If you have a family you might also ask yourself, 'How do my children see me?'.

We are going to start by looking at the attribute of a well-managed physical lifestyle. Remember, the decisions you have to make relate to minimising risk factors and avoiding hazards. Many of the desirable habits should already be in place as a result of a sensible upbringing. Thus, in relation to your own behavioural choices remember the family pattern and the need to point your own children in a sensible direction. On the whole, for example, fat parents have fat children as they all eat too much together, and the offspring of smokers and heavy drinkers may be more likely to become addicts themselves.

DIET

- Because of CHD and factors relating to obesity, diet is currently a cause of anxiety. We mostly eat too much of the wrong things.
- Diet is very much a matter of habit based on what you were taught at home. Thus, on the whole, what has not been allowed in the past is little missed today.
- There is a serious need to make our diets less indulgent, and to eat more fresh, fibrous vegetable-based foods. In view of the coronary risk it is wise to reduce animal fats and go for polyunsaturated butter substitutes, skimmed milk, cottage cheese, and so on.

Losing weight

A lot of fuss is made about weight reducing diets: for normal people weight is controlled by the calories you eat in relation to those you need for daily living. Remember that there is a variation in the metabolic rate of individuals; some burn off their calories, whereas others are good converters and store the extra as fat. Obesity is thus a credit account of calories as fat – if you start using more calories than you eat, you consume the credit and lose weight. All that is required of a weight reducing diet is that it should have – tolerably – fewer calories than you need, so that you are forced to spend your credit balance. The trick of losing weight has two aspects:

- Get on to a lower calorie (but otherwise acceptable) diet.
- Re-educate your eating habits so that this reduced intake becomes the accepted level for the future.

The long-term solution is better self-education. Starvation, as in a health farm, will drop off a few pounds quickly but it all comes back when you return to your normal way of eating.

Breakfast is an important meal to fuel up for the day, but only one main meal should follow this. The third or second should be light or low calorie. Snacking between meals should be forbidden, but if children are hungry apples, carrots, etc., are better to eat than biscuits. It is not essential to ban goodies like sweets and ice cream entirely, but they should be a *treat* and not a habit.

Remember that what you enjoy eating is very much a 'what you are used to' habit and that your digestive system is both flexible and trainable. It is wise to budget or plan your diet over a week and not necessarily for a day. Thus if there has been a heavy Monday to Friday wining and dining, go easy over the weekend. Business life is now more sensible in terms of lunching and dining, but as cost is relatively un-important it is not difficult to have steak and salad rather than steak and kidney pudding, two courses and not three, and so on. It is also sensible to have company rules about dining rooms, canteens, etc., to make over-indulgence more difficult.

Where you have your lunch and what you eat must be reflected in the family eating pattern. If one person is home-bound with children he or she may have to provide a sub-stantial main lunch, while someone who has business lunches does not necessarily need, or want, a large supper. People who live alone, on the other hand, and do not want to be bothered with cooking do need to be careful to eat enough of the right things. As a discipline they should set themselves standards to take a bit of trouble over preparing and eating their meals.

It is worth remembering two things. First, eating is a major pleasure and should be enjoyed. Secondly, the normally functioning digestive system is an apparatus designed to deal with a wide range of food simultaneously. Weight control is the most important part of diet for most of us, especially to coronary-prone people; it needs to be what the Americans call 'a prudent diet'. If, on the other hand, your LDL is low, there is no reason for not occasionally enjoying strawberries and cream.

Vitamins

Vitamins, beloved by food faddists and health food stores, are vital substances that the body needs but cannot manufacture. Thus they must be part of a nutritious diet and nearly always are. They are required in small quantities and, in spite of what the advertisements say, there is no general benefit whatever in taking extra, indeed some may even be dangerous if taken to excess. There may be disorders of absorption in the digestive system leading to deficiency diseases, but serious vitamin deficiency diseases, like scurvy, beri-beri and rickets, are very uncommon in this country.

Sensible mixed diets contain enough vitamins for all of us but older people may perhaps need a little extra in the winter. Tonics which are supposed to give lift usually contain a lot of vitamins and these mostly have a placebo effect. They are intended to improve your feeling of general well-being and very often they do because this is what is expected from them.

FOOD ALLERGIES

An allergy is an immunologically-based sensitivity to a substance which then, through the immune system, produces a violent and possibly lethal reaction. Some people (called 'atopic') are more sensitive than others. The antibodies relating to this sensitivity may be found in the blood and, as with vaccination, de-sensitisation may be possible (e.g. hayfever). The immune system is closely linked with the emotions and so stress may well play a part in setting up these allergies.

Much more mysterious is the currently fashionable cult of anxiety about sensitivity to certain foods, which may then in popular terms become 'bad' for you. It is believed, for example, that some additives may be directly dangerous and, for instance, cause hyperactivity in children. More research needs to be done on this and in the case of symptoms that do not have any other obvious cause, test-feeding may reveal a food substance that seems to provoke the symptoms. Such a sensitivity is not an allergy in immunological terms. Much remains to be found out about such sensitivity and it also needs to be established whether there are real dangers in common additives, many of which have been about for far longer than their E numbers.

The problem in rationalising the sensitivity is that people are very suggestible and follow food fads and fashions. Publicity about a food substance causing certain symptoms becomes acceptable as a conditioned reflex and may provoke the symptoms to occur in people. If you look back over ten years of food fads and fashions, they do seem to come and go like skirt lengths.

If you, or your children, have a problem which might fit into this category it is worth seeking expert advice but do not fall for the advertisements which offer to treat your sensitivities. These have been shown to be largely unreliable with results that cannot be reproduced, i.e. if you send the same sample to two different laboratories you may get two totally different sensitivities. As a last resort, particularly with children, test feeding may be desirable to identify a sensitivity – but see your doctor first.

ALCOHOL

Because alcohol intake increases insidiously (particularly if it is enjoyed and exposure is high), it is essential to have a personal discipline about how much and when alcohol is taken. Many individuals and companies would be better for cutting down regular lunchtime drinks, and there would be a good case for a weekly drink-free day for those who are socially over exposed. Some companies are much more relaxed than others and availability and precedent are factors in developing dependency. However, the number of 'dry' companies seems to be growing (perhaps under the American influence) and this may be no bad thing.

It is an interesting social quirk that, certainly in the evening, no social contact is thought to be complete without offering a drink and any gathering, even a christening, has to include one. At the same time, social pressure about drinking and driving is increasing and we are becoming far more careful about not pressing extra drinks on people who may be driving, and we should always have alternative non-alcoholic drinks available on these occasions.

Availability is undoubtedly a major factor in developing dependency, and habits, good or bad, which start young are difficult to eradicate. Controlled drinking is to be enjoyed but there must be a personal, family and company policy to set the right examples. The latter is probably the most important of all. If within the organisation the senior managers or service officers are seen to be heavy drinkers, they are copied by others. And, if the known drinkers get away with it, why should others stop?

Some companies are setting up alcohol counselling services but unless management is both seen and known to be well behind this policy, it won't work. Supervisors and colleagues know perfectly well who the heavy drinkers are. They must first be told that this will not be tolerated by the company, and then offered help. It is essential that what the Americans call 'job jeopardy' is there and that their jobs are known to be at risk. It is a good general rule, which should be emphasised to supervisors, that anyone whose performance has recently

63

fallen off or whose attendance has deteriorated should have a counselling session to find out the reasons why.

Control of drinking is very much a personal and company management problem, but it is encouraging for those of us who enjoy a drink to remember that modest drinkers live longer than teetotallers. Two or so drinks a day seem safe. Lastly, it needs to be remembered that women, probably because of their body and liver size, have a lower tolerance and can drink less. More important is the fact that alcohol should be taken minimally during pregnancy. Being in the bloodstream it gets to the foetus, and it is not unknown for babies to be born drunk.

SMOKING

A recent report claims that, for some smokers who get specific diseases, smoking can shorten life by as much as twenty years. The reasons for not smoking have been outlined in the previous chapter and it is clear that, in addition to it being personally dangerous, it is also increasingly unacceptable to non-smokers. To allow smoking or not is a personal and management decision which it will become increasingly important to make, not only at home but particularly at work. But now that smoking is a minority activity, opinion is hardening against smoking in public places. These, of course, include the work place and the reduced size smoking-zone is now replacing the non-smoking enclave. A few companies pioneered non-smoking at the work site and now non-smokers are pressing for protection as a health and safety measure.

As it is an addiction and subject to acute withdrawal symptoms, stopping smoking, for some people, can be very difficult. All sorts of gimmicks have been tried, such as group therapy (modelled on Weight Watchers), various drugs, nicotine chewing gum and hypnosis. The last of these works on some people and may be worth trying, in others group support is more helpful. A concerted attack on stopping smoking is often more effective than any attempt to cut down on alcohol, perhaps because the latter is more personality related and the drug a more obvious prop.

In the opinion of many ex-smokers, the only way to stop is to make up your mind to do so AND STOP. There is little value in cutting down slowly or waiting for the right time. There may be a case for waiting until a holiday so that you can scratch the family rather than the office. Quite a good inducement is to put the smoking money on the mantelpiece and you will soon have a sizeable 'treat kitty'. If you spend £2.00 per day on smoking there are all sorts of things you could buy with the money you save.

EXERCISE AND ENVIRONMENT

- Keeping moderately physically fit has an emotional as well as direct physical effect. Also being active is an attitude of mind as well as a discipline, i.e. walk some of the way to work, don't always use the lift, go and see people rather than waiting for them to come to you in your office.
- Exercise should be regular, brisk enough to get you slightly breathless and put up the heart rate, and be overall mildly demanding. A twenty minute walk each day will do you more good than you might believe.
- There is no one form or ideal way of taking exercise, but there are advantages in outdoor activity, and, for the busy person, doing things with the family or in groups over the weekend has additional advantages.
- Now that children seldom play organised games or even do much gym at school it would seem sensible to

encourage one's children by example, to build exercise and fitness into their lives.

- If you are physically tired, you sleep better in spite of any anxieties. In fact, physical fatigue is a good antidote to anxiety.

Feeling fit, well and not sluggish is something to be enjoyed and, for the workaholic particularly, time spent exercising is legitimate time away from the 'phone. Being willing to take regular exercise is an attitude of mind which makes a major contribution to well-being. You don't have to go to a gymnasium to walk upstairs briskly – how many people could run up two flights without puffing? If you have a disability, say an arthritic hip or vulnerable back, it is essential to keep up muscle strength in the rest of you. This is particularly true of backs which get more vulnerable if the muscles weaken.

In America there has been a recent development in the provision of supervised gymnasia for the use of managers and other staff in office hours. In this country a few companies have copied this practice and there is at least one organisation – Fitness for Industry – which will advise and provide fitness facilities. There are also, of course, many businesses that are situated in areas with good access to public or commercial facilities for physical recreation.

It pays company management to have a positive attitude to fitness and to encourage fitness in all its staff. Like everything else it should start at the top and in general terms include weight control and non-smoking. If there is any sort of company medical service this should include health education and counselling.

SUMMARY

- The principal decisions to take about our physical life-style are all about minimising the risks.
- The key areas which are under our day-to-day control are diet, smoking, drinking, and exercise.
- Diet needs to be carefully watched particularly with the easy availability of 'junk food'. A well managed diet can make you well.
- Losing weight can only be achieved by cutting down on calories and re-educating our bodies that fewer calories are the norm.
- Drinking in moderation does little harm; smoking is harmful with absolutely no redeeming features.
- Regular exercise can be very beneficial and the best motto is 'little and often'. A brisk twenty minute walk each day can work wonders.

CHAPTER FIVE

UNDERSTANDING MENTAL HEALTH ————————

INTRODUCTION

In the previous chapter we looked at the areas of our physical lifestyle which are under our control and the actions we can take to limit the risks. In the area of mental well-being, the options are not always as clear. We can measure the fact that we may be overweight but how do we assess our mental well-being in an objective way when the condition may rule out any possibility of our being objective in the first place?

What is, however, important is not to imagine that there can be a division of lack of well-being into the physical and the mental. All lack of well-being can be the symptoms of an underlying dis-ease, and is just as likely to be the manifestation of mental illness (e.g. anxiety and depression) as it is to be the physical symptoms like headache, backache and indigestion.

This chapter sets out to do two things. First, it will attempt to clarify the issue of mental illness, which is still veiled in ignorance. Secondly, it will cover in more detail one of the areas that leads to mental dis-ease; a breakdown in relationships. This may sound a little far-fetched but one of the defined causes of mental ill-health is an inability to maintain satisfactory social relationships.

The busy executive may be so engrossed in work that he neglects his home life – to the eventual detriment of his marriage. His wife has not been able to cope with the drifting apart or with her 'failure' to match her lifestyle with that of her husband's aspirations. The husband himself may have set out on a career which has turned sour or where his ambitions have not been matched by opportunity or personal attributes (we can't all be Managing Director). Now, older and perhaps wiser, he finds it difficult to re-balance his lifestyle and build up satisfactory relationships in areas possibly outside work.

And, for husband and wife, read wife and husband. More and more women demand their own career and they are just as vulnerable to the general unhappiness and frustration that can follow a poor balance between office and home and between ambition and ability.

BACKGROUND

In recent years, significant mood change – anxiety, depression, phobias, insomnia, irritability and so on – has been accepted as being just as real reflections of dis-ease as the more traditional symptoms of dyspepsia or asthma. In today's climate, with 30 per cent of marriages ending in divorce, children running away from home and massive consumption of tranquillisers, there must be something wrong with our mental health and emotional control.

These may appear to be minor matters when compared with the overt and often uncontrollable behaviour disturbance involved in manic depression, schizophrenia and the like, but the whole spectrum of mental disease is important as a cause of disruption and reduced performance. Some of it is genetically determined and runs in families as a strong tendency. There is often a shared environmental factor, with a parent expecting you to have the same symptoms as they did, like migraine or a weak stomach. This is known as the inheritance of acquired characteristics.

Mental ill-health is misunderstood. We all too often believe it to be restricted to the more extreme forms of behaviour found only in 'mental homes' like the man who believes himself to be Napoleon. But mental illness is *far* broader than that and comes in all shapes and forms. It can range from anxiety and loneliness through to such things as drug and alcohol abuse, compulsive gambling and severe depression. It is no respecter of status or background; none of us is immune.

For the individual, it means a major impairment to comfort and happiness; for those close to the sufferer it is seen as a major impairment to efficiency and social well-being. It affects people at home, and it affects them at work. Most people, if they had to choose, would prefer a physical disability to one which could eventually destroy their powers of thought and reasoning. Yet mental illness is an area of medicine that is still veiled in ignorance and suspicion and, all too often, guilt. The reluctance of Jane Smith to lift her portable computer because of a bad back will arouse understanding and sympathy. Her reluctance to come to work at all because of an 'inability to cope' would all too often be regarded as a sign of weakness – both by her employer and by herself.

Nevertheless, the reality is that mental illness, in all its forms, is widely believed to be one of the single greatest reasons of absenteeism caused by illness not only of the people at work, but also of their families. Time off work due to stress-related illnesses is estimated to have increased by 500 per cent since the mid-1950s and now costs industry hundreds of millions of pounds a year. The cost is even higher if we take into account the effects on British industry of drug and alcohol misuse. Our dependency on soft drugs (such as tranquillisers) is growing all the time; the effects of alcoholism have been estimated to cost the country at least £1.7 billion a year. And these are *known* statistics; the guilt factor has not been taken into account. For every known abuser of drugs or alcohol, for every person who is known to suffer from psychological or emotional problems, there are countless people in employment who are frightened to tell of their problem or who refuse to acknowledge it or seek help.

It is difficult to get precise figures for the incidence of mental disease, particularly for the common and neurotic conditions which are largely dealt with by GPs. In terms of the spectrum of dis-ease already discussed in holistic terms, the presentation of symptoms is, in any case, hard to define accurately. However, the latest figures produced by MIND, the National Association for Mental Health, show that at any one time 250 out of every 1,000 of the population consult their GP for some form of mental distress. Seventeen of these will require specialist advice.

Looking at more serious mental disease, national figures from the Government show the hospital admission rate for mental illness (including long-stay serious and chronic cases) is 417 per 100,000 of the population in 1986. In 1976 it was 385. The incidence for women only is 486 per 100,000. There is no doubt about the seriousness of mental illness.

WHAT IS MENTAL ILLNESS?

In general terms, mental illness is experienced as a significant impairment of comfort and happiness, evidenced by a falling off in efficiency or in the capacity for satisfactory social relationships. The range of symptoms is very wide and extends from conditions which are sufficiently severe to call for hospital treatment through to ones which, although less severe, may nevertheless be significant sources of personal unhappiness and social inadequacy.

Mental health is not a category – it is a spectrum. At one end we have the absolute ideal of health with complete emotional stability, no neurotic feelings, personal happiness and good relations with family, work and society. Few people are ever in that ideal state and if they are, they're rarely in that ideal state all the time. In the middle of the spectrum are varying degrees of unhappiness and difficulties in coping, and at the end of the spectrum is what most people would regard as 'true' mental illness, e.g. schizophrenia.

The mentally healthy person copes with life and its problems without undue distress and without causing undue distress to others. Even when under pressure, he or she remains able to recognise what the problem is and to deal with it without losing self control or the ability to respond in an adaptive and coping way. An inability to cope (i.e. stress) is therefore a manifestation of mental illness.

Although many people believe that mental illness is on the increase, there is no good evidence for this. Life has always been difficult and there have always been people who have failed to respond to the challenges of life: the evidence now is that there is more help available and so more people are asking for help. At the same time, there is little evidence that city life is more stressful than rural life, or that life in a developed country is more stressful than life in less developed countries. Stress is fashionable, but it is not the preserve of the harassed business executive. There is documented evidence that, in a community in North West Africa the daily round of getting enough food to eat is so difficult that the people show all the symptoms of (and are being treated for) stress. There is a high incidence of both major and minor mental illness in such communities even though their way of life may sometimes seem desirable when compared to our own.

THE DEFINITION OF MENTAL ILLNESS

One of the problems with defining mental illness is, of course, that we must first define what constitutes 'normal'. We can say with some certainty that a normal human being has two arms and two legs; anybody without his or her full complement of limbs could safely be described as 'abnormal' in this context. But when we are dealing with something as complex as behaviour, normality is very difficult to define. Not only that, normality has to be viewed against the background in which the behaviour is being judged. What may pass for normal behaviour in Brixton might not necessarily be viewed in the same light in, say, Cheltenham. Also, we have to be careful not to impose our personal standards when checking normality; other behaviour can be perfectly normal, in its context, even though it may offend us personally.

By the generally accepted definitions, abnormal behaviour leads to problems of mental illness when there is a failure to adapt to society and when such failure of adaptation causes either social nuisance to others or distress to the individual concerned. Such distress usually arises either from inefficiency at work or from an inability to make or maintain satisfactory social relationships.

Mood varies all the time and covers a spectrum of emotional feelings. Clearly too, the expression of mood relates to personality; the taciturn, the changeable, the bubbly outgoing, and so on. Stress thresholds also vary but stress such as grief or anxiety will also influence mood. Thus there is a constant fluctuation of mood and feeling which relates to personality, life situations, general health, and stress, all of which constitute a spectrum of what might be called normal reactions and responses. In this spectrum it is normal and sensible to be elated, depressed or anxious, tense, and so on, even a bit manic if over-excited.

Clearly, there is nothing abnormal in suffering from swings of mood. Everybody has mood changes from time to time but the danger signs are when these mood changes become prolonged and have no obvious cause. Excitement, for example, occurs in all of us and normally for short periods, but if it occurs as the main feature of a person's behaviour, in the total absence of any outside cause, and is sustained over a considerable period of time, then it is a manifestation of mental illness.

Likewise depression. It is quite normal to be depressed when life is difficult and depression could be quite severe and prolonged following a death or a major financial reversal, for example. But if it occurs as a main feature in a person's behaviour and is out of all proportion to any apparent outside cause, then it has a pathological basis.

Mental illness can therefore be defined as the state when depression, anxiety, mania, and so on become entrenched to the extent that they modify normal behaviour and response. The two commonest are depression (the tendency to which may be inherited) and anxiety states, both of which, when severe, can seriously limit normal reactions and relations. Phobias, like the fear of going out, are a limited form of anxiety whereas paranoia and panic are extreme forms of what can be quite normal reactions.

It is usual to try to divide depression into endogenous and affective. The former, which is often inherited, is said to come from inside you and seems essentially to be a brain malfunction, whereas the latter is a reaction to the more unwelcome events which life occasionally has in store for us.

Modern drugs (antidepressants and anxiolytics) (when skilfully manipulated) often produce dramatic cures but do not really deal with the cause. Shock therapy is available for severe and suicidal depression.

This rather simple outline applies to 'neurotic' bahaviour. Diagnosis can be complicated for both this and 'psychotic' conditions which can arise from lesions within the brain (as with a stroke or cerebral tumour) and even as a reaction to certain drugs. Reactions to serious and possible terminal disease can also produce similar behaviour disturbance.

Severe and more debilitating psychotic behaviour follows much the same spectrum, with schizophrenia, manic depression and acute mania being the most common. It may sometimes be difficult to make a precise diagnosis of a particular psychosis but this is outside the scope of this book.

ANXIETY AND DEPRESSION

In terms of a doctor, a supervisor or a relative trying to help someone who is either anxious or depressed, it is often difficult to decide the most appropriate approach or treatment. This is made particularly difficult because both terms – anxiety and depression – are frequently loosely used without the distinction between a symptom and a diagnosis being realised. Both states involve serious mood change, which is in any case constantly fluctuating in a healthy individual.

A further difficulty in classification or assessment for treatment lies in the fact that the precipitating factor may be totally genuine, like bereavement or redundancy. Thus, just as a serious headache is a manifestation of some other cause – e.g. a fever or even a brain tumour – anxiety may legitimately arise from a lifestyle crisis.

If overt anxiety or insecurity is a major disability or symptom, it is essential to treat the cause rather than to 'tranquilise' the symptom, although the latter may have a legitimate place in the short-term restoration of stability. It must also be remembered that the symptoms may arise from a basic weakness of personality or other emotional condition, such as a phobia or fetish. Against this background, it could be argued that an acute panic attack or anxiety state is a disease rather than a symptom but this is a technical problem for the psychiatrists.

Depression describes a change in mood leading to doom and despondency, and may be the result of inherent changes in the brain or a reaction to external events. But depression can also be brought about by conditions causing extreme lethargy and is characterised by inability and unwillingness to concentrate, sleep disturbance, and even delusions or suicide.

Not all depressed patients admit to overt depression, blaming their symptoms on the overlying disease of the body, rather than the mind. Viral infections, alcohol, malnutrition and other diseases can trigger this off. Here again the doctor has to decide what to treat but it should be remembered that depression can be an upset in its own right and need specific treatment. But because of their protean nature, depression and anxiety are under-diagnosed and sufferers are either exhorted to 'pull themselves together' or are given tranquillisers, to which they may well become addicted.

Currently in Britain we have what appears to be a mini-epidemic of the ME syndrome (myeloencephalitis), which often follows a viral infection and produces long-lasting weakness and lethargy.

What is important is that the symptoms of anxiety and the condition of depression, particularly in the milder forms, are relatively common. They both cause loss of efficiency and well-being and are often badly handled by supervisors and doctors. Their existence must be suspected and accepted and appropriate treatment instigated. Always remember, however, that even quite extreme mood swings are part of life and a legitimate reaction to real problems. A holistic analysis may well be better than a prescription.

Paraphrasing what Churchill said about his depressive phases, 'the black dog of depression has sharp teeth', it must also be accepted that in the mood swings of manic depression the manic phrase can be uniquely creative, particularly for artists.

DEALING WITH THE PROBLEM

Dealing with any problem depends largely on two factors: first, knowing that the problem exists – is a real problem – and second, learning to recognise it – by its effects. This is particularly true of mental disease often experienced as anxiety and depression. To be dealt with, mental illness first has to be accepted as a possible disease and then recognised and properly treated.

It is usually difficult for the 'patient' to make his or her own diagnosis, at least the first time round, but partners and supervisors can pick up the signs and instigate support, understanding and treatment.

Depression, for example, means what it says; the sufferer is *depressed*, gloomy and miserable – ask them and they will often admit this predominant mood. This leads to two sorts of symptoms. First, the inability to face up to major problems and make decisions. Like the alcohol dependent, the depressed or over-anxious busy themselves with trivia. Essentially, there is a marked deterioration in 'performance' at work and at home. Second, there is an alteration in the sleep pattern, not of difficulty in getting to sleep but with early waking and gloomy thoughts, described by Churchill as 'the black dog'. Recognition and acceptance are the first steps towards coping.

In all of this, one of the major determinants of recovery is the way other people react to the sufferer. If depression results as a reaction to a major change, the sufferer often feels guilty, believing that someone of more 'moral fibre' would not have succumbed. Part of the difficulty faced by people being treated for any kind of mental problem is that they believe it is in some way their fault. Mental illness still has a stigma and while we never accuse people with diabetes (suffering from a lack of a chemical required by the body to break down sugar) as being the victims of their own folly, we still enquire of the person in depression, 'what have you got to be depressed about?', as though the chemical inbalance leading to mood change were in some way his or her fault.

Detailed diagnosis is very much a matter of judgement, and is very dependent on good rapport between doctor and patient and the willingness of the former to ask questions about personal problems. Studies by psychiatrists of seriously ill patients in medical and surgical wards have shown that many of them have mental symptoms of this type, which delays their recovery. This is a reaction to their disease, the problems of which have not been explained to them. A lot of anxiety ferments because of ignorance and perhaps a bit of paranoia – conditions which are not unknown in the executive suite.

A key to maintaining a fair mental balance is to try and

realise how all these forces interact, to know your own personality, strengths and weaknesses and to be honest about your tensions and difficulties, and also to be prepared to discuss them with somebody else. If in fact you get physical symptoms or even behavioural ones with no apparent cause, don't rush to the medicine cabinet but sit down and try to analyse where the stress is. Regard the symptoms as a friendly devil, warning that you are up against your stress margins in some sphere.

Very often, such are our personal defences, cause and effect are much more obvious to outsiders and family. The important thing is to pick these reactions up early and discuss them before they get institutionalised and over-rationalised. Also, because it is defensive, some people are successful because of their neuroticism, which becomes a protective shell behind which they function more effectively. Finely-balanced people carrying a heavy load may find that the treatment is worse than the disease, and so they put up with the symptoms. It is not unknown for people to handle a highly stressful situation successfully only to succumb to depression when the stress is removed.

COPING WITH STRESS

The underlying assumption behind all of this is that stress is a reaction to too much challenge for you at a particular time. It relates to your personality, your various skills and experience, your aspirations and your attributes. It is a reflection of your life-pattern and not just a part of you. Understanding the parameters of health and dis-ease and being determined to maintain both your own and your family's well-being is obviously a major step towards stress management, but it doesn't guarantee a place at the top of the stress avoidance league.

The digestive system can, given the right minimal ingredients, rebuild the dietary intake into the substances required for energy, growth and maintenance. It is fairly flexible and can accommodate frequent changes with no obvious problems. Mental health may well be less flexible, so that disturbances of behaviour (genetic or acquired), personality traits like anxiety, introversion or a type A personality, have to be accommodated as they cannot often be totally overcome: they do impose restrictions on performance and influence behavioural reactions.

The most important thing about coping with stress is to register there is a problem and then to look for the possible causes of conflict. People are surprisingly reluctant to do this and plough on for months or even years in the same confused state, hoping that something will turn up and solve the problem. It must be realised that 'causes' relate as much to personality as they do to external events. As genetic inheritance is a common risk factor, your personality can be regarded as the denominator of the equation and assessed objectively, i.e. you have to recognise and live under terms which are largely dictated by the person you are.

Not being able to make up one's mind on a course of action – about a situation or relationship – is often because of an unwillingness at least to define the alternative options. It requires training – in getting the right management information – to see the need for this. Once the options are known, the best or least dangerous option can be chosen. Again, as with management, there may be an element of risk-taking in adopting the most attractive option, like getting out of an uncongenial situation. On the whole, though, fortune favours the brave (and backing your judgement is highly motivational).

It may well be that, at the end of the analysis, there is no alternative but to plough on, at least for the time being. But at least the analysis has been made and the compromise accepted cheerfully. You can then get on with life having decided against the alternatives. Very often, the mere fact of listing the causes of the problem and the options available clarifies the stress and makes it easier to live with.

Defining the causes and selecting the options is the first and main part of managing the stress problem and it involves honest objectivity. Related to this is the willingness, and again the need for objectivity, to seek advice from a friend, counsellor or even expert. They may well point out to you that the situation you are in is largely your own fault and that you had better mend your ways. Experience does show that a problem shared is one that is well on the way to solution. If you have a personality difficulty, like anxiety or tension, an expert – medical or paramedical – can teach you coping skills.

This is called stress counselling. The other thing that a stress management counsellor will do is to help you identify and analyse the events in your personal and business life that are paticularly stressful and teach you 'pre-stress' preparation and related relaxation techniques, to minimise the tension. If you do find certain aspects of life difficult, it is well worth seeking help from a clinical psychologist.

Stress and worry produce tension which consumes energy tightening muscles, and limiting clarity of thought. Over-reaction of this type is not the same as becoming beneficially 'psyched-up' and getting the adrenaline running for a diffi-cult situation. It is a classical harmful over-reaction, perhaps more flight than fight.

There is now a range of relaxation techniques available: the process of relaxation can be learned and is thoroughly beneficial when incorporated into your lifestyle. It also helps to improve the quality of sleep. The two best known methods are probably Transcendental Meditation (TM) which is largely auto-hypnotism, and Yoga. There is a range of others going from relatively straightforward self-help methods like autogenics and bio-feedback, to learning a simple regime which suits you. Like many complementary therapies, no one method is universally applicable and it is sensible to find the one that suits you best and easy to learn.

There is also an admirable organisation called Relaxation for Living which offers advice, supplies tapes and literature, trains teachers and runs classes in relaxation. It is effective in its approach and has a critical over-view of the various methods that come and go. Because drug dependency – particularly of tranquillisers – arises from continued use, they are also interested in helping people to break the drug

habit. They see relaxation as very much a part of stress management.

There is also a lot of benefit in following a sensible basic regime for keeping healthy. A very simple one was covered in the television series produced some years ago by Thames Television called 'How to Last a Lifetime'.

- Try and avoid serious fatigue. If you do find yourself getting over-tired, then you should take immediate steps to overcome it by resting and reducing work load.
- Keep a good balance between rest and activity.
- Take plenty of physical exercise.
- Try and ensure that you get enough good quality sleep.
- Whatever you're doing, plan it and plan it in a way that gives you plenty of time to reach your deadlines with targets that can be reached with confidence.
- Try and keep some energy in reserve.
- When things get on top of you, and people are demanding too much, learn to say 'no' (and learn to say 'no' to yourself as well).
- Learn some relaxation skills and practice them as often as possible, particularly when you are in a situation that you know produces stress and worry for you.
- Finally, know your own personal limitations and keep within them (which is another way of saying 'learn to say no').

If you add to that the recommendation to have a regular check up and to develop a healthy balance between work, play and family, you have the basic rules of survival for most of us.

SUMMARY

- Mental ill-health can cause a breakdown of relationships, and *vice versa*.
- Mental health is misunderstood and affects far more people than we might imagine.
- Everybody has changes of mood – mental ill-health is manifested by periods of mood change becoming prolonged with no obvious cause.
- The most common manifestations are anxiety and depression – both often brought about by prolonged stress.
- Coping with stress means coming to terms with our own limitations to handle the challenges – not necessarily for reasons in our control.
- Learning to relax is one of the best safety valves.

CHAPTER SIX

FAMILY AND WORK ————

INTRODUCTION

We have seen that stress is known to play a great part in cardiovascular disease of one sort or another (and remember that this is the western world's top killer disease, far above cancer). Heart attacks used to be blamed solely on our dietary habits and our sedentary lifestyle until it began to be realised that there was a third major component – the stresses and strains we accumulate every day of our lives. These can take us into a state of exhaustion and then tip us over into complete physical breakdown. But it is not only heart disease that results from stress. Doctors have established a long list of disorders in which stress is a major contributory factor, ranging from insomnia to backache, high blood pressure, arthritis, and certainly to mental illness, i.e. across the whole spectrum of disease.

The circumstances that produce stress-related illnesses are many and varied. Two researchers, Holmes and Rahe, looked at the events in our lives which required us to make re-adjustments of one sort or another, both major and minor, and gave each one a score. They found that anyone who totalled over 300 points in a year had an 80 per cent chance of succumbing to illness. The points allocated to each event range from 100 at the top to 12 at the bottom (the mark given to Christmas, and on the low side because we presumably get over it fairly quickly!) The top ten items on the list with their scores are as follows:

Death of spouse	100
Divorce	73
Marital separation	65
Jail term	63
Death of close family member	63
Personal injury or illness	53
Marriage	50
Getting the sack	47
Marital reconciliation	45
Retirement	45

It can therefore be seen that out of the top ten crises in life which required some kind of readjustment, eight involved some degree of breakdown in our relationships, both at home and at work. Consequently, establishing and maintaining good relationships can have a major impact on our well-being, certainly as far as the majority of us are concerned.

DEALING WITH RELATIONSHIPS

While it is true that one of the manifestations of mental illness is the failure to handle social relationships successfully, it is equally true that such a failure (in developing social relationships) can play a part in increasing our vulnerability to mental problems. And, in many cases, it is our family relationships which are the most important because they can often be an escape route from our work problems. A well-balanced home life can provide the safety valve for work problems and help us to keep them in perspective.

There will always be a few exceptions but for most of us our well-being depends on leading a balanced life, in which challenge and satisfaction come from several sources. Also, for most of us, the main sources of pleasure and satisfaction come from work and relationships, at home, at work and in a wider field. Stress and conflict will arise from failures in these areas; success, on the other hand, can be very conducive to our well-being.

A large part of the grid against which we measure our behaviour and reactions is determined by our cultural inheritance, and varies around the world. Within this there is room for deviations that are tolerated in a reasonably flexible society. Obviously this flexibility is the spice and variety of life, as without it we would all be boringly the same. Consequently, the way we live is made up of a series of individual habits, conditioned reflexes and beliefs which make us feel better by providing a reason for what we do. We may be subject to fashions which seem odd to others or which have no apparent rational basis, but, provided they fit the general definition of 'normal', there is no problem. The way we develop our relationships with other people, however, depends on a greater level of acceptance and understanding of our 'normality' and on our acceptance of theirs.

THE BASIS OF GOOD RELATIONSHIPS

Some people may drift satisfactorily through life and into relationships without much apparent thought or policy. They may have luck and good judgement. But for most of us it is sensible to have a personal policy about how we want to live, where we want to get to and what relationships we need or want. It is sensible for these targets to be realistic and subject to periodic review in the light of experience. Throughout the whole of our lives, our aspirations and attributes have to be in balance to avoid stress.

A person and a family benefits in three ways; first, by understanding the ground rules of their chosen lifestyle; second, by being honest enough to be objective about their personality and problems; and most important, third, to be strong enough to discuss problems rather than to bottle them up, and to seek advice where necessary. Basic outlines of living sensibly have already been discussed, as has the need for and value of leading a diverse and balanced existence. Single-track people may be outstandingly successful but they tend to be bad at relationships and are vulnerable.

Relationships are critical for most of us and are often badly handled, with disastrous results. We tend to take them for granted, drifting along hoping there will not be a crisis. This attitude, however, must reduce the quality of life in which relationships are tolerated rather than appreciated. And, of course, when there is real conflict the stress is tremendous.

THE FAMILY

We start our adult life with an inheritance of genes, experience and beliefs from our childhood. We may accept and agree with these or find them unsuitable for our aspirations, and go our own way. Biologically, there are no reasons why families should stay in touch – the young are reared and pushed out into the world to do their own thing – but obviously there are, for most of us, benefits in family continuity and solidarity. It is worth, therefore, having a framework on which to build your family life in the future.

First, you need a family programme for bringing up your children, with rules and sensible disciplines but also with considerable freedom and understanding to let them be themselves and not mirror images of you. Forcing children to over-achieve can be very damaging and destroy self-confidence. Bringing up children requires insight, understanding and patience. Some parents handle their children very badly and even as grandparents may not always approve of the way which their children react to their grandchildren.

Children mostly manage to survive, provided the discipline is consistent and not unpredictable.

Secondly, we need to end up with a good relationship with our adult children. We have to resist the temptation of treating them always as 'children', expecting both obedience and gratitude. 'All we did for you, dear', constantly reiterated, is not the basis for a relationship. 'Mum and Dad' become a duty rather than a pleasure to their children.

Thirdly, (and overriding all of the above) is the need for a strong basic relationship between partners, whether this be in or out of wedlock. Many of us seem to drift into marriage or partnership without really thinking through why, or what we expect to achieve from it. For a partnership to be rewarding there has to be enough in it for both people to be satisfied and rewarded. Meaningful relationships between intelligent in- volved people are difficult and require periodic renegotiation if the relationships are to survive. Needs, priorities and personalities change with the various phases of life.

Underlying all this is the fundamental need for everybody to understand the basis on which his or her family life is going to run, and to re-assess it continuously over the years. You don't expect your working life to stay static (people come and go, companies develop, markets change) – why should your home life be any different?

THE NEED FOR BALANCE

The inevitable conflicts of career and home life must be faced objectively and talked through thoroughly. The British are not good at discussing personal problems, so irritations fester and become grievances. Well-being does very much demand openness and if necessary willingness to seek counsel- ling advice over problems.

The work ethic for professional and managerial people

does make for over-ambition and the desire for the status of being high up the ladder. We fail to realise that the majority of us constitute the average and that we cannot all be outstanding. If only we could accept being ordinary, and perhaps not drive our partners to over-achieve, we might be happier and less confused. Mid-life is very much the time to reassess totally our aspirations and attributes with honesty and objectivity. It is also the time, perhaps, to stop trying so hard, accept being average and develop some outside interest which may become more satisfying than work. In fact there is nothing more stimulating, if one is brave enough, than the challenge of a quite different, and perhaps less demanding, role.

The statistics do not lie – we spend far too much time in the doctor's surgery looking for cures for illnesses which are essentially due to our own behaviour. The people who allow their work to take over their lives, who fail to maintain a balance between ability and ambition, neglect their partners and their families, and who have no interests outside their work, are putting themselves, their partners and their children at risk. It may take years to surface but the gradual build up of a stressful background with no escape routes can lead to a breakdown of the mind which is just as much an illness as chicken pox or measles, and which may need to be treated in much the same way – with drugs and careful nursing.

But the causes are much more difficult to establish and need a reassessment of the *way* we run our lives and what we expect out of life. This requies a much more honest approach to self-assessment than going on a diet or cutting down on alcohol. But it has be done.

MANAGING YOUR CAREER

This book is not the place for a treatise on management theory but it is the place for emphasising the key points about anybody's career. A successful career means facing up to the challenges of daily business life. A healthy company will find out what its managers are made of by judiciously exposing them to challenge and seeing how they cope with it. A healthy company will also ensure that its people end up doing jobs at which they are comfortably competent, and do not end up on the scrap heap.

But challenges which cannot be met are a cause of stress, and stress is probably the number one affliction of the workplace today. The remainder of this chapter is not on how to deal with stress, rather it covers the areas (at both a personal and company level) that may help stress to be avoided or at least minimised.

The personal level

- There are horses for courses. At any stage in your career, you should be able to look around and say to yourself, 'Is this really what I want? Is it what I am best at?'.
- In managing your career, you have to make choices, to know when to change jobs and, basically, to discover whether you are a large or a small company person. Entrepreneurs, for instance, seldom do well in the often civil service-like bureaucracy of a large organisation. Conversely, gifted people who create a successful organisation often come unstuck when, because of growth, they have to find themselves working as part of a team.
- As well as being challenging and creative, management is inevitably competitive because it is, by definition, hierarchical. There can only be one boss. Nevertheless, the successful company also depends on teamwork and leadership at every level to provide job satisfaction to everybody regardless of their ambition. Consequently,

92

successful managers are often those who manage to blend their own attributes and requirements with those of the company.

- Successful managers accept that they cannot be all things to all people, nor can they do everything most of the time. If things are urgent and you can't deal with them, then they have either to be delegated or ignored.

- Delegation is seldom a natural gift and, indeed, many people think of it as a sign of weakness. In fact, it is a sign of strength and security. If you enjoy doing the job yourself, delegation is the art of enjoying seeing it being done well by somebody else.

- Delegation is the way to bring on younger people. Just as you enjoy the challenges of daily life, so do they.

- Keep a balanced lifestyle; work isn't everything. One partner often puts up with separation because of the career needs of the other, which leaves them isolated. Children tend not to know a busy working parent (it is often said that executives keep photographs of their families on their desks because they tend to forget what they look like).

- Get enough exercise and get enough sleep. Short-term 'fire-fighting' can be exhilarating but not when it becomes a habit. Take your holidays and try and avoid delusions of indispensability. The company will survive perfectly well without you for a short spell of time.

- Go back to the first point and ask yourself, 'Is this really what I want?'. The most successful managers are those who have achieved a balance between work and leisure, who are working within the limits of their capabilities, and where the challenges they face can be coped with.

The company level

- People are a company's most valuable and least replaceable asset. They are probably the only asset in the company's balance sheet which isn't written off or otherwise depreciated. It has been said about many companies that if the management took as much trouble over their staff as they did about money, they would be twice as well off.

- All members of a company need to know what is expected of them, what their job entails, and to have a clear idea of their objectives and responsibilities. It is said that one of the most stressful aspects of work is not knowing what you are really meant to do and not knowing on what basis your job is going to be measured. The second most stressful aspect is knowing all this but then not being allowed to get on with it.

- Communicate with your staff. Every company has its own system of communication. It will either be on the informal level (the grapevine) or on a more formal level. Where companies set up effective and fast means of communicating with their staff, then communications will be good. Where they ignore the need for a formal system of communication, then an informal system will be set up and communications will be bad. Whether you like it or not, your staff will receive communication by one means or another – it is up to the company to decide the quality of that communication.

- Keep in touch with your staff and know what is going on. If things are going wrong with their performance, it is nearly always due to some form of stress. Depression and anxiety in moderate and severe forms produce the same indecision, unwillingness to delegate and an inability to grasp nettles. People bury themselves in trivial detail and become too busy to do anything properly. They don't take holidays and they go home late.

- Time has to be spent in face-to-face communication. This doesn't mean endless indeterminate meetings, which can become a way of life; it means an environment in which anxiety, frustration and criticism – at all levels – is presented and openly discussed. It requires a degree of maturity for the company to accept criticism, but it makes for all round better performance and job satisfaction.

- Keep people on the move. Boredom is a prevalent form of stress, in terms of lack of challenge, particularly in middle management. While it may be convenient to keep someone in a job they know (for you, not them), a sideways movement may well re-invigorate them. A rule of thumb is that no one should stay in the same routine job for more than about five years.

- Read the first point again. Looking after your staff is to take good care of your most valuable asset. There is nothing wrong with being a demanding employer or manager, but that doesn't mean being uncaring. Some of the companies which stand head and shoulders over others in Britain, as far as good management practice is concerned, apply nothing more than basic common sense when it comes to determining the environment in which their staff work.

ONWARDS FROM FIFTY

Retirement is one of those times in life which actually leads to stress, so being better prepared for retirement is very much a part of managing our health. A lot of preparation must be closely linked to work; more people than ever before expect their income in retirement to be linked to their employment (through their pension) and more employers are recognising that they have a major role to play in helping people move out of employment and into retirement.

About twenty-five years ago people began to realise that, because of the increase in the number of retirement-aged people, retirement was a new social problem to be thought about. In those days the retired had little status, nobody wanted to know them and the majority had inadequate pensions. The retired were poor and disregarded and, because of their lack of status, they were effectively 'non people'.

From this rather gloomy viewpoint has emerged the belief that if you are going to live another twenty years in reasonable health, retirement needs both planning and preparation.

The foundation was thus laid for the now rapidly expanding network of 'preparation for retirement' training courses, run publicly and by companies.

Modern thinking about retirement now sees it as twenty years or so of new challenge and opportunity, during which people should do enjoyable things free from the diary and financial worry. But it does require self motivation and considerable thought.

Over the years, of course, private pensions have improved, largely through the spread of occupational pensions and without the need to pay the NI contributions, pension contributions and possibly a mortgage (plus the fact the children have grown up and probably left home), the need for income is nowhere near as great as it was when we were working. Health and life expectancy have improved, more people are living longer, so that 25 – 30 per cent of the population are retired and want to go on making a contribution to society. The final removal of the earnings rule in 1989 makes part-time work much more financially rewarding and the younger retired can mostly find paid work if they want it.

A changing pattern

Of course, the basic concept of retirement was, and still is, that it should be recreational but, within recent years, major changes have begun to occur.

- The number of younger people entering the work-force is falling and there is going to be labour shortage, particularly of skilled and professional people. The gap between supply and demand has to be filled by somebody and this is leading to job opportunities for older people (who are, in any case, often perceived as being more reliable employees than the young). America has raised its retirement age, with MacDonalds, for example, employing older people in preference to younger ones. In this country a large DIY chain has just opened a major branch, staffed entirely by men and women over 60, with appropriate training available.

- There is a growing feeling that management life, being what it is, will lead to careers peaking at 50+, at least for senior people. Also, the less senior are beginning to be encouraged to consider either a sideways move (to be more stimulated) or to change course entirely and do something quite different, more exciting but perhaps less demanding.

This new challenge is exciting and, rather than thinking of retirement as recreational, the idea of a different career might become popular. Thus there will be opportunities to work differently but in a constructive and contributory way from, say, 50 to 75. This activity would not necessarily be fully salaried but some opportunities might well be.

Overall, it looks very much as though the concepts of retirement and its financing are about to change. Being formally retired or being an elderly pensioner may no longer be expected, at least before 75. People will change gear and role in late mid-life to enable them to go on doing meaningful and useful things for very much longer. The concept of a life based on a single skill could well disappear, as more flexible attitudes towards skill requirements emerge. Indeed, a society with, at most, 40 per cent of its potential workforce actually creating wealth (with the rest either being trained or retired), may not be economically sustainable. Whether they like it or not, older people, over the next twenty years may have to give up the concept of formal retirement between 55 and 65. Planning for all the aspects of a different life after 55, will be an exciting new challenge for those sensible enough to promote and preserve their well-being.

Time planning

When retirement comes at no matter what age, the problem of how to spend it and what to do with yourself and your partner has to be looked at under several headings.

- Although it marks the end of one phase of life, it is more importantly the start of a new one which may last many years. It requires as much thought and planning as did

97

the choice of and preparation for a career.

- There is the need for time planning: what are you going to do, how will you fill your diary? Work confers status, identity and association with other people. The trick of retiring successfully and growing old gracefully is to develop a new and meaningful persona and if necessary a new social network.

- Activity can be paid or unpaid, full or part-time but it is important to think through how much time partners want to spend together, and how much separately. You may not want to be under each others' feet all the time. In any case, there is more to talk about if you do different things.

- Where will you do all this? The same house? Different house? Same location? Somewhere new? It may well be that because the house will now be fully occupied, it needs to be bigger; having individual territory reduces the possibilities of friction. Particularly in retirement each member of the household requires 'nag proof' territory.

- Do not forget financial planning; make your money serve your priorities. Planning must be flexible, expert and ongoing. It must also be joint planning and based on open discussion to minimise anxiety. Women live longer than men and are thus more likely to be left on their own. They need to know what they will have to 'cope' on. Not knowing is a major source of anxiety.

- Finally, but most importantly, there is, of course, the maintenance of well-being to maintain health. Providing the right challenge and satisfactions will help you to get the maximum benefit from your earlier investments in health and well-being. There are also some simple health rules for older people which help the process of growing old gracefully.

It is worth remembering the quip, 'If I had known I was going to live so long, I would have taken more care of myself '. This book should help you to do just that: *living sensibly is prudence and not hypochondria.*

SUMMARY

- Some of the potentially most stressful events in our lives involve a breakdown in relationships.
- Relationships are often taken for granted but they usually need working at.
- The basis of family life is not constant, it needs re-assessing on a regular basis.
- It is important to create a balance between family and work.
- At work we need to keep our own careers under review to make sure we are working sensibly and effectively – and happily.
- Companies should ensure that their staff are working in a way which optimises the balance between self-fulfilment and meeting the company's objectives.
- Preparing for retirement is an essential activity when we are in our early 50s, although changing demographic patterns might lead to a new look at employment in later life.
- Retirement can be a success but only if we work at it. We rarely plan to fail – but we often fail to plan.

CHAPTER SEVEN

WOMEN'S CONCERNS

INTRODUCTION

In these days of sexual equality and equal opportunity, it may seem a little odd to have a chapter in any book devoted especially to women. In terms of their aspirations, women are no different from men when it comes to determining their lifestyle and attitudes. In their general approach to health management, therefore, men and women need the same information and opportunities. In the workplace, the position is changing and equality of opportunity is soundly based on the essentially sensible premise that there is really no difference at all between men and women.

But that is not true in the area of health. No matter how ardently you may support the premise of sexual equality, there is no avoiding the inequalities of biology. Pretending otherwise is a mistake for both men and women, indeed, 'vive la difference'.

There is absolutely no doubt that there are health differences between the sexes. Of course, women have hearts, lungs, guts, brains, etc. the same as men and are equally vulnerable to conditions such as arthritis, colitis, sinusitis – you name it, women get it. However, not only is there little evidence that women consult their doctors more frequently for these con-ditions than their male counterparts, there is actually a survey (Gallup poll: Nov. 89) which showed that women workers took fewer days off work than men – seven days a year compared to twelve days a year for men.

Not only are women generally healthier than men, they also live longer (about six years on average) and this increased lifespan is seen throughout Europe. This is one reason why their pensions are smaller (the same size of fund cannot afford to pay an identical income for, on average, a further six years) and why they pay less for their life assurance.

However, if women generally enjoy better health than men, why does the statement 'female employees in Great Britain are more likely than males to have been absent from work through sickness in the week studied' appear in *Social Trends*? There are several explanations for this and it is reasonable to look at the problem from two points of view – women as women, and women as carers.

WOMEN AS WOMEN

Women have been blessed with a reproductive apparatus that needs regular maintenance. This apparatus can – and does – malfunction and causes symptoms from time to time that require investigation. Women have little or no choice in this matter; rarely would they choose to get fibroids or ovarian cysts or other reproductive problems.

Women are more often than not responsible for contraception, which may involve visits to the doctor for regular checks and monitoring.

These situations mean women inevitably visit their doctors more often than men and, as their reproductive careers are usually over by the age of fifty, these visits are concentrated in their early working life.

The overall result of all this is that a good part of the disease in women is due to their unique differences when compared to men, i.e. their reproductive system. It is also the aspect of their lives where good health management can pay dividends later on. For all the joy that childbirth can bring, the reproductive system is prone to problems, many of which can be modified by regular health care.

SCREENING

It is important to ensure that the reproductive system is kept as healthy as possible. Breast examination, cervical smear tests and pelvic examinations are the platform on which this good health is based.

Breast screening

- There are 25,000 new cases of breast cancer each year in the UK. One in every twelve women will get this disease. We cannot prevent breast cancer, and the risk factors we know about – family history, age, reproductive history – cannot be altered. (See Table 8.)
- The majority of lumps in the breasts do not matter at all and could be safely left for a hundred years without giving any problems. Unhappily, one in ten of these lumps in older women is likely to be caused by cancer.
- Screening for breast health comprises of three separate examinations. Breast self-examination, a clinical examination by a healthcare professional, and breast X-rays – mammography – in older women.
- Self-examination every month enables a woman to find abnormalities of her breasts early so that she can seek her doctor's advice as soon as possible after the lump is discovered.
- A clinical examination can be properly carried out either by a doctor or a specially trained nursing sister, both of

whom need to have training in the special skills necessary for this examination.

- Regular mammography examinations should be carried out from 40 onwards and will detect the majority of breast cancers. Mammography is a special X-ray examination used to find early cancers which cannot yet be felt by either the woman herself or by anyone else. It also helps in the diagnosis of palpable breast lumps.
- Mammography is not perfect. It will pick up many women who do not have cancer but who have some other innocent condition of their breasts. These women will need to be recalled for further breast examination or follow-up X-rays, which will obviously be worrying.

Because neither mammography nor clinical examination *prevent* breast cancer, it is important to carry out breast self-examination in the interval between formal screening examinations. This is why monthly breast self examination is so important and can help in the early detection of cancer.

Table 8 Deaths in women under 65: England and Wales, 1988

	Numbers	Percentage
Heart attacks	5982	15.2
Cancer – breast	5372	13.6
– digestive Organs	3525	9.0
– lung	3072	7.8
– reproductive organs (uterus, cervix and ovary)	2874	7.3
Stroke	2601	6.6
All deaths under 65	39439	100

Source: OPCS DH2 89/2

The cervical smear test

- This test is designed to find *pre*-cancer changes on the surface skin of the cervix. It is *not* a *cancer* test. Large numbers of women have these pre-cancer changes and probably only one in three of them would ever develop invasive cancer of the cervix even if they never had any treatment at all.
- If every sexually active woman had a regular smear test every one or three years from the age of twenty and had proper treatment if an abnormality was detected, then her chances of getting cervical cancer would be reduced by over 90 per cent.
- Cervical smear tests can be carried out by General Practitioners, Family Planning Clinics and Well Woman Clinics, either in the public or the private sectors.

Pelvic Screening

The womb, ovaries and the Fallopian tubes (which run between ovaries and the womb) all live in the pelvis. Three tests can be used to identify any problems here.

- *Physical examination* by a nurse or doctor may identify problems of the womb (such as fibroids) and problems of the ovaries or Fallopian tubes which can result in swellings such as ovarian cysts or blocked and swollen tubes.
- *Ultrasound examination*: high frequency sound waves can easily identify enlargements of the ovaries and ultrasound is being explored as a possible way of early detection of ovarian cancer. Again, it has the common disadvantages of screening in that many women are identified as having enlargements of the ovary that turn out not to be cancer. The only way to exclude cancer is by abdominal surgery – laparoscopy (looking into the pelvis by a tube) or laparotomy (a formal surgical operation).
- *Blood tests* for cancer are also being tested out. One test –

CA125 – is used to screen for ovarian cancer and it is proving useful but not perfect. Maybe a combination of tests will prove to be the best way forward.

Enlargements of the womb found on pelvic examination are almost always innocent. The most common abnormality is fibroids.

REPRODUCTIVE HEALTH

Monthly problems

Like every mammal on earth, women have a regular ovulation cycle. However, only women (and some monkeys and apes) have a regular cycle associated with loss of blood. For women it is an inconvenience which can range from temporary discomfort to real distress. Not without good cause have women sometimes referred to their period as 'the curse'.

This book is not intended to be a medical dictionary but is designed to explain (particularly to men who are largely unaware) that many things (including, for example, stresses, accidents, or even aeroplane travel) can cause disruption of this finely-balanced mechanism.

- *Pre-menstrual syndrome (PMS) or pre-menstrual tension (PMT)*: almost every woman experiences some symptoms before her period starts and, in some, these may cause distress. PMS is almost always associated with ovulation – that is, it indicates that the ovaries are active. A doctor may be able to suggest ways in which this can be suppressed by using hormones. Vitamin supplements can also be useful in the treatment of PMS.
- *Painful periods* in young women usually relate to uterine 'spasm'. Doctors are not entirely sure why. Suppressing ovulation seems to help but if periods become painful in

later life it is usually due to some disorder of the womb or ovaries and should be checked out.

- *No periods (amenorrhoea)*: severe stress, bereavement, or severe weight loss can abolish periods, as can excessive exercise.
- *Heavy periods*: each month the average woman loses a relatively small amount of blood. Its loss usually causes no problems at all but by definition not everybody is average and some women find that the blood loss does interfere with their normal daily life. Excessive loss can be controlled by hormones or by taking iron tablets to correct any anaemia, but in all cases, it is important to find the cause, and the lining of the womb may need to be checked by a D & C. If that does not solve the problem, the treatments then are using hormones (for younger women) or a hysterectomy – removing the womb altogether (but usually keeping the ovaries). A new operation called 'endometrial resection' may be an alternative. This is where an electrical wire loop or a laser is used to destroy and remove most of the lining of the womb. This operation only requires a day or so in hospital, compared to at least five days for a hysterectomy, and recovery is rapid. It is an operation that many women would choose in preference to a hysterectomy.

Problems of the cervix

Cervical erosion, or as it is more properly called 'cervical ectopy' usually gives no problems at all. The delicate tissue of the lining in the canal comes to lie on the outside of the cervical canal. This delicate lining produces a lot of mucus and in this new vulnerable position it is prone to infection. A simple cauterisation of the cervix is usually all that is necessary to eliminate the troublesome symptoms this causes.

The menopause

Every woman experiences the menopause, the vast majority in the years between 45 and 55. While 'menopause' usually relates to the cessation of periods, women who have had a hysterectomy experience this anyway as a result of losing their womb, though they may be far from menopausal in age. Menopause treatments are now widely available and are given for two reasons: to relieve menopause symptoms; and to protect bones against osteoporosis.

Symptom control

The most effective way of relieving symptoms is to take hormones, a treatment which is now widely known as hormone replacement therapy (HRT). The hormones in question are either oestrogen or progestogen. Oestrogen alone is usually more effective than progestogen alone though women who have not had a hysterectomy should take both in order to prevent build-up of the lining of the womb. This can happen with continuous oestrogen treatment and is *possibly* associated with the later development of cancer of the lining of the womb.

The disadvantage of this combined treatment is that the majority of women continue to have regular monthly periods. This may be a joy but is more often considered a disaster and is certainly one of the main reasons why many women avoid HRT. Before starting HRT, it is wise to have a thorough check-up which should include a cervical smear, pelvic examination, mammography and blood pressure checks. This examination should be repeated regularly at least every three years and preferably every year.

Osteoporosis

Thinning of the bones is common in older men and women. It is more important in women because they live longer and their bones are thinner than men's, even when they are healthy young people. A woman is more likely to develop osteoporosis if she is a white, non-exercising smoker of advancing years, whose mother had osteoporosis, who had a childhood or adolescent diet poor in calcium and vitamins and who doesn't take HRT.

From this you can see that HRT is only one facet of the problem of osteoporosis. At least two-thirds of post-menopausal women will not have osteoporosis of a degree significant enough to influence their life or health. Not smoking, eating a good diet and exercising regularly through-out life are every bit as good as HRT in preventing osteo-porosis in old age.

Mid-life transition

The menopause happens at a bad time in a woman's life. The mid-life 'itch' affects both men and women. Dissatisfaction with self, job, home, partner, life difficulties with ageing parents, rebellious teenagers, personal health, it is all there in the middle of your life, along with, but not *because of*, the menopause. Menopause treatment can help the symptoms of the menopause but it won't stop Johnny taking drugs or Grandma going demented.

WOMEN AS CARERS

Women are often seen both by themselves and others as being the major carers in their family. This is the area where statistics can be slightly misleading, because the statement we included at the beginning of this chapter includes the words 'absent from work through sickness', which do *not* simply cover those times when women have been ill them-selves. Our culture seems to expect women to be the family nurse regardless of who is ill. Single women, even if they have full-time jobs, are seen by married relatives as having plenty of free time to look after mother or father. Mothers are expected to see to their children's immunisations and take them to the doctor when they are ill. It is estimated that almost one quarter of all women's visits to the doctor are on behalf of someone else – a child, husband, parents, in-laws or neighbours.

The previous chapter discussed the changing shape of the population. People are living longer, and older people are more susceptible to illness and so more likely to be dependent on others. Whether or not there will be a change in the role of women in taking care of dependants remains to be seen. If women expect a greater role in the world of work there seems no reason why men should not expect to have a greater role in the home.

Caring has a place in this book because understanding the problem – the challenge – is to cope with it and coping with challenge means avoiding stress.

Coping with common serious diseases

Once a serious disease has been diagnosed and the appropriate treatment started, which may involve stability rather than cure, it is sensible to assemble the facts and to review the options. These will obviously vary with the nature of the disease and the public and personal resources locally available.

You should find out all that you can about the condition, ask questions, find people who have had it and above all, find out if that disease has any supporting Association. For instance, organisations like the Parkinson Disease Society, the Diabetic Association, the Alzheimer Disease Society, and many others, provide not only information but support and encouragement through local groups. The College of Health will, through its advice lines, be a good starting point for information.

Often this is more useful for chronic disease, those causing long-term disability or disabling conditions, congenital or related to birth. With regard to some severe disabilities of this type it does require ruthless objectivity to hold a balance between the needs of the carers, the rest of the family and the sufferer.

Cardiovascular disease: CHD or stroke

Only about one-third of coronary attacks are immediately fatal so, in any one statistical year, there will be twice as many more coronaries as coronary deaths. After a coronary much can be done to reduce the chances of its recurrence. Obviously the immediate outlook hinges around the extent of the arterial blockage and the possibility of arterial replacement or other unblocking measures to improve the situation.

Within about a year of a mild coronary, a normal life with considerable physical activity can be expected. Immediate rehabilitation will include supervised physical activity, with the body's own reaction being a good guide. There is no place now for turning people into invalids by telling them to 'take it easy'.

Medical advice will also include a review of risk factors and the adoption of a better lifestyle if necessary, in terms of smoking, weight, diet, exercise, etc. More important, however, is for the patient to sit down and analyse, with their partner, the factors which might have made them a coronary risk. If they want to survive they may well have to start again and stop being a type A personality or being quite so ambitious.

The severity of a stroke depends on the precise injury to the brain and on the general state of the patient, i.e. an obese person with possibly other diseases finds getting movement back much more difficult. Recovery can be very slow, particularly if speech is involved, and it depends on the determination of the patient and the encouragement and support of the family. Professional physiotherapists can help with special exercises but so can everyone else, particularly with speech, by firm help and encouragement. There is also a range of electronic gadgets for helping communication, turning on TV sets, etc. The Chest, Heart and Stroke Association can be generally helpful about all the problems involved with strokes and heart attacks.

Cancer

Although it is regarded as a killer, it must be emphasised that about half of all cancer is successfully treated, and, further, that a patient's attitude and approach can, in some cases, promote this success and may limit secondary spread. You should throw into gear any family contingency plan there may be to cope with serious and possibly fatal illness. Any plan should be based on openness and honesty with no attempt to pretend to the sufferer that recovery is likely if the opposite is true.

Most people prefer to end their days at home but it is essential that adequate domiciliary support is available, including expert nursing. It is equally essential that the carers get enough rest. As part of this a decision has to be taken, with medical advice, as to whether terminal care should be at home with domiciliary hospice support, in hospital or possibly an in-patient Hospice unit.

The Hospice movement is a prime example of a major facility being developed in the voluntary sector. It is a continuing care service, firstly helping sufferers come to terms with the diagnosis of serious disease and then helping with the control of pain and other symptoms which may, or more usually may not, develop later in the disease process if it is incurable. Its success is based on two separate approaches, both equally important. The first is the adequate control of pain. If the patient knows that there will be no pain more things can be contemplated with much less anxiety. The second is the philosophy of openness, buoyancy and support from family and staff. All the patient's questions must be answered honestly; there should be no deception between family and patient. The Hospice movement also provides continuing support for relatives after death to counsel the bereaved.

Hospices are now quite widely available and are even being built on NHS land. Some areas which do not yet have a Hospice building start by providing a domiciliary service. Along similar lines, the Macmillan Nursing Service and the Marie Curie Foundation also provide skilled domiciliary nursing support. There are also helpful Societies like the

Breast Cancer and Mastectomy Association, and the Stoma Association, where people who have been treated will come and talk to patients before an operation and reduce the mystery and anxiety by describing what it is like and the quality of life afterwards. BACUP is a clearing house for information on cancer treatment and care.

Chronic and increasing disability

In terms of the individual and family hardship, chronic and progressive diseases which lead to mobility and social problems (like Multiple Sclerosis or mental illness), are much more difficult to adjust to. You will require knowledge of the condition and its natural history, and knowledge of and ability to obtain your entitlement from the Social Services, as well as adequate medical support. There is an active Carers Association with local groups and, as with other conditions, a specific Society can be very helpful, as can MIND for mental illness, and MENCAP for chronic mental disability.

Elderly relatives

Now that more people are living for longer, most of us are faced with the problem of elderly relatives. At least one fifth of the over 85s will be mentally confused before they die, adding another dimension to the problem. There are now also many frail couples who can no longer cope and who need domiciliary support, so special housing for the frail elderly is beginning to include married accommodation as well as single flatlets or rooms.

Local Authorities – now the Social Services – have a legal responsibility to provide the frail elderly with accommodation and domiciliary support, but this is often deficient or institutional. A bewildering range of special allowances is available for the frail elderly but these (together with domiciliary support and respite for carers) may not be readily available in every area. Specific advice from the Citizens' Advice Bureau (CAB) may help you to get the best out of the resources available.

Facilities vary across the country and local availability could be a factor in deciding where to live. Organisations like Age Concern, GRACE, Care and Advice for the Elderly, and the College of Health supply guides to what is available, where and at what cost, on a local basis.

Dementia and confusion

After fear of getting cancer, the second most common fear that haunts us as we get older is fear of confusion or dementia, particularly so if we have had to help cope with a confused elderly family member. Confusion, which is sometimes called senile dementia (or pre-senile dementia if it came on at an earlier age), begins when parts of the brain cease to function properly. As with other forms of severe mental disturbance, confusion can also be caused by organic brain damage, drug toxicity or overdose and alcoholism, but mostly it comes in two forms which have recently been separated out. These are Multiple Infarct Dementia and Alzheimer Disease.

Multiple Infarct Dementia (MID) is a manifestation of generalised arteriosclerosis where 'mini strokes' knock out groups of cells in the brain. It is not necessarily progressive but deterioration may come in waves and it comes on later in life. It is largely due to wear and tear and treating the hypertension (which causes arteriosclerosis) may hold it at bay.

Alzheimer Disease (AD) seems to be a specific disease entity with characteristic cellular changes in the brain (it is currently thought that aluminium may play a part in this causation). It may come on earlier, is more rapidly and inevitably progressive and sometimes seems to run in families.

The borderline between mild dementia and engaging dottiness may be hard to define. Failure of short-term memory is a normal age change but what happens in dementia to cause confusion is that the memory or part of it goes. This is disturbing to the individual who loses touch with the here and now and may have only one thing in their mind at a time and infuriates everybody else by following them around asking the same question repeatedly.

Mild forms of dementia can be coped with at home but it is very demanding. As with other forms of disability the needs of the carers are ongoing and just as important as those of the patient. There is a growing number of special units in the private and public sector, with access to the latter being mostly means-tested. Standards, particularly of Local Authority units, are improving as all these homes have to be registered and are regularly inspected.

Grief and bereavement

The British are particularly bad at dealing with bereavement which is, after all, an inevitable problem we must all cope with sooner or later. The process of grieving follows a more or less set pattern and has definable stages. There are also accepted counselling patterns to ease and explain progress through the process.

Sadly, it is usually considered that the demonstration of grief should be bottled up. Other cultures benefit enormously by being allowed to demonstrate their grief publicly and get it out of their system. Nevertheless, while it is natural to want to mourn it is equally essential that it should not go on for too long. Successful mourning should result in 'healthy remembering' which becomes a stepping stone to re-entering productive life.

The main stages of mourning are; first, shock, disbelief and an inability to accept what has happened; second, pain, guilt, sad acceptance, depression and difficulty in coping with life; and, third, gradual acceptance and return to normal life. Mourning is made much harder to bear by the physical and mental loneliness. Bereavement counselling consists of a shoulder to lean on, someone to talk to (and if necessary to cry with), plus the general and social help and encouragement which makes life much more bearable. Bereavement counselling services are available in many areas and organisations like CRUSE exist to help.

We ought all to be aware of the need for bereavement counselling. Understanding the inevitability and naturalness of grieving helps recovery, but in coping with bereavement, as with·other emotional problems, we need maximum openness and minimum bottling up. If steam is let out explosions are less likely to happen.

MOTHER AND MANAGER

The decision to have children in today's society is a very different matter than it was only 30 or 40 years ago. Then, it was expected that the mother would give up work and devote herself full-time to bringing up her family. Today, the decision to have children is often taken against a background of a successful career for both parents, with women insisting that their desire to start a family need not mean abandoning this career. Even where they prefer to give up their job, women now look for greater assistance in moving back into employment when their children are at school, and do not expect to take a back seat in deference to the fathers in the office.

It is possible – but not easy – to combine children with a career. Well over three quarters of married adults believe the best arrangement for children under five is for their mother to be with them full-time. Even when considering children in their early teens, most people think that the mother should work part-time only. Less that 1 per cent of married adults consider that the under fives are best cared for by both parents working full-time, and even for young teenagers only 15 per cent of married adults believe both parents working to be the best arrangement.

So the working mother already flies in the face of this rather entrenched opinion which says she should not be working. These opinions may work against her career progress quite irrespective of any other factor. Yet the very opposite attitude is embodied in the Employment Protection

Act 1988, which lays down the rights that all women have regarding maternity benefit, paid leave and the right to return to work six months after delivery. This gap, plus pre-maternity leave, keeps many women away from their jobs for some nine months at a time, and this in itself can be very career limiting. It is also very difficult for any company to lose a key person for this length of time. Changes happen and companies develop in this timespan and it is very tempting for the woman manager voluntarily to reduce her maternity leave in order not to miss out on her career. Many self-employed women with no financial cushion of maternity pay take little time off after childbirth.

Nevertheless, make no mistake about the natural bonds that are forged between mother and child. Nature is not stupid. She realises how time-consuming and demanding a baby can be and without the bond that makes each mother devoted to her child it would be so easy to give up on this helpless creature and abandon it. Few women – of whatever occupation – have not shed a tear on leaving their child to return to work, and few mothers have not longed to remain at home with a sick child, even though there was excellent help available at home.

Balancing the demands of home, family and career is not easy and, indeed, no one pretends it is. Today's husbands and fathers are much more aware of the problems than before and many are prepared to play their part in home making and child rearing. But for most women, the sign over the door is 'The Buck Stops Here'. They will be the ones to organise the housekeeper, the baby-minder, the shopping and the sickness care.

Career breaks/maternity leave

Once a woman has decided to have children and becomes pregnant, she may well be entitled to return to her place of work six months after her baby is born. However, more and more employers are understanding that this is not always a practical solution or even one that is desired by the mother. These companies are exploring the possibility of *career breaks*

117

where a woman is given up to five years leave of absence and then offered her employment again at a similar grade. This career break involves the employee working for at least four or possibly eight weeks per year full-time for the company to keep up-to-date with new working practices and technology.

This approach has proved very successful in retaining skilled women workers and reinforcing their bonding to the company. However, a recent survey by the British Institute of Management stated that, although more than half the women managers who had taken an extended career break had used it to advance their careers through training or other means, companies were singularly lackadaisical in maintaining contact with their women managers during these extended breaks. Only 4 per cent of companies offered organised updating seminars, refresher and retraining courses.

Creches/nanny vouchers

Creches are provided by many large companies. Alternatively, several small companies working in the same geographical area can combine to support a creche. An alternative to this is the provision of *nanny vouchers* available to either men or women employees, a system that is up and running in the United States. The vouchers are made out like cheques to the carer with registered child minders, nurseries, nannies, au pairs or even relatives being eligible for this scheme. However, the vouchers are not tax-free although they are exempt from National Insurance.

The Government's white paper 'Employment in the 1990s' states that employers can no longer treat women as second-class workers. Employers must recognise that they do not only need women but they must also recognise women's career ambitions and domestic responsibilities.

SUMMARY

- Women are generally healthier than men. They certainly live longer (about six years on average).
- They also, paradoxically, have more time 'off sick' due to the fact that they are women and their role as carers.

Women as women . . .

- Women's reproductive systems are a source of frequent discomfort and potential illness. Regular screening is good health management, particularly in older women.
- The menopause can be a difficult time but modern treatment (e.g. HRT) can help reduce the symptoms.

. . . as carers

- Women have a traditional role as carers and usually take the leading role in coping with serious illness.
- Understanding is the prerequisite of coping. Well over half the sufferers of really serious illness survive with good nursing and careful rehabilitation.
- Terminal illness needs careful counselling – before and after the patient's death. The Hospice movement is a powerful force in terminal care.
- Looking after confused elderly people is likely to become an increasing feature of care in the future.

. . .and as mothers

- The majority view is that mothers should look after their very young children.
- More companies are making it easier for women to return to work by introducing career breaks, creches and nanny vouchers.

Women are different from men. They may certainly have different skills and applications in the workplace but they also perceive themselves – and are perceived by society – as having different roles and responsibilities from men in the home. Their bodies are different too. Women cannot be held personally responsible if their bodies fail to function in the ideal way.

In general, however, their health has greatly improved and would appear to be better than that of men. At the turn of the century, average life expectancy of a live born girl child was some 47 years. It is now 78 years. It is estimated that by the mid 1990s, 50 per cent of the workforce of Great Britain will be women. It is important that employees and employers together work out a strategy for using this workforce successfully, productively and without harming the basic family unit as we presently know it, and which is the mainstay of our society.

Fredrick Nietzsche said, 'From a woman you can learn nothing of women', while Otto Weininger said, 'No-one who is not female can be in a position to make accurate statements about women'. So men don't agree either. But my money goes on Otto!

USEFUL ADDRESSES

Age Concern England
Bernard Sunley House
60 Pitcairn Road
Mitcham
Surrey
CR4 3LL

Tel: 071–640–5431

Alzheimer's Disease Society
158–160 Balham High Road
London
SW12 9BN

Tel: 071–675–6557/8/9/0

Arthritis and Rheumatism
Council (ARC)
41 Eagle Street
London
WC1R 4AR

Tel: 071–405 8572

BACUP (British Association of
Cancer United Patients)
121–123 Charterhouse Street
London
EC1M 6AA

Tel: 071–608–1661
Freeline: 0800–181199

Alcohol Concern
305 Gray's Inn Road
London
WC1X 8QF

Tel: 071–833–3471

Anchor Housing
Anchor House
269a Banbury Road
Oxford
OX2 7HU

Tel: 0865–311511

Association of Community Health
Councils for England and
Wales
30 Drayton Park
London
N5 1PB

Tel: 071–609–8405

British Association of
Psychotherapists
c/o 121 Hendon Lane
London
N3 3PR

Tel: 071–346–1747

British Diabetic Association
10 Queen Anne Street
London
W1M 0BD

Tel: 071–323–1531

Cancer Care (Marie Curie
Memorial Foundation)
28 Belgrave Square
London
SW1X 8QG

Tel: 071–235–3325

CARE (Cancer After-Care and
Rehabilitation Society)
21 Zetland Road
Redland
Bristol
BS6 7AH

Tel: 0272–427419
0272–232302

Chest, Heart and Stroke
Association
Tavistock House North
Tavistock Square
London
WC1H 9JE

Tel: 071–387–3012

Disability Alliance
25 Denmark Street
London
WC2H 8NJ

Tel: 071–240–0806

Hospice Information Service
St Christopher's Hospice
51–59 Lawrie Park Road
Sydenham
London
SE26 6DZ

Tel: 071–778–9252

British Heart Foundation
102 Gloucester Place
London
W1H 4DH

Tel: 071–935–0185

Cancer Relief Macmillan Fund
Anchor House
15–19 Britten Street
London
SW3 3TY

Tel: 071–351–7811

Carers National Association
(Formerly Association of
Carers and National Council
for Carers and their Elderly
Dependants)
29 Chilworth Mews
London
W2 3RG

Tel: 071–724–7776

College of Health
18 Victoria Park Square
London
E2 9PF

Tel: 071–980–6263

Disabled Living Foundation
380–384 Harrow Road
London
W9 2HU

Tel: 071–289–6111

MENCAP (Royal Society for
Mentally Handicapped
Children and Adults)
123 Golden Lane
London
EC1Y 0RT

Tel: 071–253–9433

*MIND (National Association
for Mental Health)*
22 Harley Street
London
W1N 2ED

Tel: 071–637–0741
Contact Information Unit

*National Association of Citizens
Advice Bureaux*
115–123 Pentonville Road
London
N1 9LZ

Tel: 071–833–2181

*Parkinson's Disease Society of
the UK Ltd*
36 Portland Place
London
W1N 3DG

Tel: 071–255–2432

*REACH (Retired Executives
Action (Clearing-House))*
89 Southwark Street
London
SE1 0HD

Tel: 071–928–0452

*RNIB Talking Book Service
for the Blind*
Mount Pleasant
Wembly
Middlesex
HA0 1RR

Tel: 071–903–6666

*Multiple Sclerosis Society of
Great Britain and Northern
Ireland*
25 Effie Road
London
SW6 1EE

Tel: 071–736–6267

*National Council of
Psychotherapy and
Hypnotherapy Register*
c/o Stream Cottage
Wish Hill
Willingdon
East Sussex
BN20 9HQ

Tel: 0323–501540

Patients' Association
18 Victoria Park Square
Bethnal Green
London
E2 9PF

Tel: 071–981–5676
071–981–5695

*Relate: National Marriage
Guidance*
Herbert Gray College
Little Church Street
Rugby
Warwicks
CV21 3AP

Tel: 0788–73241

*Women's National Cancer
Control Campaign*
1 South Audley Street
London
W1Y 5DQ

Tel: 071–499–7532

INDEX